TALES OF HAZARD

TALES OF HAZARD

Being the personal narratives of ten men who have hazarded their lives in the carrying out of some important work or in some notable adventure

Edited by H. C. ARMSTRONG

Tales of Hazard was originally published by John Lane The Bodley Head Ltd in 1932 shortly after the original BBC broadcasts.
This edition follows the text of the first edition with minor emendations and a revised selection of photographs.

The preface is copyright of Colonel John Nicholas Blashford-Snell CBE.

All rights reserved.
Hardback ISBN 978-1-7391597-2-6
Paperback ISBN 978-1-7391597-3-3

No part of this book may be reproduced in any form or by any electronic or mechanical means, including information storage and retrieval systems, without written permission from the publishers, except for the use of brief quotations in a book review.

This edition published in 2022 by Daredevil Books.

Every effort has been made to contact all copyright holders. The publishers will be pleased to make good any omissions or rectify any mistakes brought to their attention at the earliest opportunity.

Daredevil Books is the home of classic accounts of derring-do from the last century. We create new illustrated editions of often hard to find iconic books that explore the feats of the brave and daring on land, ice, sea and in the air. For more information about our current books and plans for the future please visit us at www.daredevilbooks.co.uk

www.daredevilbooks.co.uk

ORIGINAL EDITOR'S NOTE

In the summer of 1932 the British Broadcasting Corporation organized a number of broadcasts under the title of the Hazard Series. Each broadcast was given by a man who had, either in Peace or War, hazarded his life in some notable adventure or important work.

This series of broadcasts created a great deal of interest among the listening-in public, and The Bodley Head decided to publish the broadcasts in book form.

The broadcast arranged to be given by Captain Hashagan has been included though its actual delivery was cancelled for reasons of international policy, which, though of importance at that moment, have now ceased to have the same value. Captain Hashagan has therefore written what he had intended to say.

I am indebted to the British Broadcasting Corporation, to Messrs. Christy & Moore, Ltd.

H. C. ARMSTRONG

PREFACE

These are tales of courageous men who faced great danger. I have always believed that to display courage one must experience fear and without doubt these brave men must have overcome a fear.

There are two types of courage, physical and moral. Physical courage is an emotional state that drives one to risk injury or death but the moral variety will often lead one to make an unpopular decision or stake all against one's own judgement. Strangely, those who appear to possess unbounded bravery do not always display moral courage. On the other hand I have never known a person who has moral courage to be found wanting in the face of physical danger.

The tales tell of those who appear to have faced danger with both types of courage and who had the willpower to press on whilst still being conscious of the need to care for their colleagues. Without doubt they had a spirit of adventure and discipline but above all they possessed courage.

These inspiring stories are worth bearing in mind as our world becomes even more hazardous from climate changes, disease and conflict.

Colonel John Nicholas Blashford-Snell CBE

Colonel John Nicholas Blashford-Snell CBE is a former British Army officer, explorer and author. He founded Operation Raleigh and the Scientific Exploration Society and is one of the world's most renowned and highly respected explorers. He has mounted more than a hundred expeditions over the past 50 years all over the world, concentrating on scientific research and community aid.

FOREWORD

All people with imagination have their dreams. The sailor longs 'for a tall ship and a star to steer her by'; the polar explorer, in the comfort of his home, hears the call of the frozen wastes, the soldier thinks back to the comradeship of the battlefield.

These 'Tales of Hazard' sound a call to all to go adventuring and the call is all the more thrilling because of the note of reality in every story.

You will find bravery in these tales. Once, in 1912 on that vast plateau which surrounds the South Pole, I said good-bye to five men. Within memory no men have faced what those five endured on their long nine-hundred-mile march back from the South Pole. Biting blizzards, driving snows, hard ridges of wind-swept ice, yawning crevasses, exhausted them, and the pitiless cold ate into their bones and starved and numbed them with agony.

But they fought their way back northward with unfailing tenacity. First died Seaman Evans, and then Captain Oates who, when he realized that with his frost-bitten feet and hands he could not hope to win through, deliberately walked out on to the great ice barrier into a blizzard and gave his life for his companions; and last died Scott, the great leader, with his companions-undaunted to the end.

You will find, in these tales, also the comradeship of adventure. Once I stood on the bridge of a light cruiser with a captured German U-boat captain beside me. I had been shepherding a convoy of food ships and he had been working to torpedo them. Between us there was no hatred. We had rivals; but we were fellow craftsmen who had shared the thrill of Hazard.

In this book men who served with us and men who fought against us have recounted their adventures, simply and at first hand.

And you who read will realize that it was not all success, but that often behind all the effort lay disappointment and depression, even failure; but the reward of adventure lies in the thrill of the Hazard.

E. R. G. R. EVANS, CB, DSO

CONTENTS

ORIGINAL EDITOR'S NOTE	V
PREFACE	VII
FOREWORD By Vice-Admiral E. R. G. R. Evans, CB, DSO	IX
I. IN SEARCH OF THE SOUTH POLE By Vice-Admiral E. R. G. R. Evans, CB, DSO	1
II. COURTING DISASTER IN MYSTERY SHIPS By Rear-Admiral Gordon Campbell, VC, DSO, MP	19
III. IN THE DEPTH OF THE SEA By Kapitän a. D. Ernst Hashagan	37
IV. TWENTY-FOUR HOURS IN THE FOREIGN LEGION By Major P. C. Wren	51
V. THE FIRST SUBMARINE PASSAGE OF THE DARDANELLES By Commander H. G. Stoker, DSO, RN	69
VI. ROUNDING UP THE TURKISH BRIGANDS By Captain H. C. Armstrong, OBE	91

VII. FACING DEATH ON THE   107
    GEORGES SHOALS
By Weston Martyr

VIII. LOST IN THE JUNGLE   127
By G. W. T. Garrood

IX. BOMBING ENGLAND   147
By Kapitänleutnant a. D. Joachim Breithaupt

X. TEN THOUSAND MILES IN THE SADDLE   167
By A. F. Tschiffely

THE 'HAZARD' BROADCASTS   185

I
IN SEARCH OF THE SOUTH POLE

By VICE-ADMIRAL E. R. G. R. EVANS, CB, DSO

EVANS OF *THE BROKE*

EVANS, VICE-ADMIRAL E. R. G. R. Born in 1881. Went from the *Worcester* direct into the Navy in 1897. He was attached to the Antarctic Relief Expedition in 1902; and served as Second-in-Command to Captain Scott in the Great Expedition to the South Pole in 1912. During the World War he commanded destroyers and, as Commander of the *Broke*, with her consort the *Swift*, in April 1917, he engaged six German destroyers, of which *Broke* sunk two and drove the remainder to flight.

Since the War, he has commanded a cruiser in China, the battle cruiser *Repulse* and the Royal Australian Squadron. He has been awarded the CB, both civil and military, the DSO, three medals for saving life at sea, and many other medals and decorations.

Vice-Admiral Evans has just been appointed to be Commander-in-Chief, Africa Station.

IN SEARCH OF THE SOUTH POLE

I WILL ASK YOU TO put the calendar back twenty years – to the time when the late Captain Scott was starting for that great sledge journey to the South Pole which ended in both triumph and disaster. My own part in that memorable journey was to pioneer the way and to bring back the last supporting party from almost within sight of the Polar area itself.

On October 24, 1911, four of us left our base at Cape Evans with two motor tractors dragging six sledges and a weight of nearly three tons of provisions, stores, pony food and petrol. The object of sending forward such a weight of stores was to save the ponies' legs over the variable sea ice, which was in some places hummocky and in others almost too slippery to stand on. Also, the first thirty miles of barrier was known to be bad travelling and to be crevassed in all directions, so here again it was desirable to save the ponies and allow them to march light and unhampered.

We had a pretty rough time with the motors, because in those days we understood little about air-cooled engines. We had frequent breakdowns and trouble with overheating, and finally, after conveying the three tons of stores a distance of fifty-five miles, the motors broke down hopelessly and had to be abandoned. We in the motor party proceeded to drag nearly 800 pounds' weight to a position in latitude 80° 30° south, where we had been ordered to await the arrival of our leader and the main southern party. We made such good progress over the ice that we reached the rendezvous six days before Scott, but we heard afterwards that he had been delayed partly by bad weather which we had escaped.

We must surely have been the first in the world to spend a week holiday-making on that frozen Sahara, the great ice barrier. We employed our time, whilst waiting for Captain Scott, in building an enormous snow cairn to mark the 80° 30' depot. The number of hours given to this kept us very fit, and our leisure time we spent in the fur sleeping bags while Day, our motor engineer, read *Pickwick Papers* aloud to us.

November 20 found us growing impatient, but at last relief from our inactivity came. Just before 5 a.m. on the next day we heard shouts and, popping out of the tent, found Captain Scott's party of ten men leading ponies, followed by two more with the dog teams. The pony leaders looked tired, and we looked as though we had come out of a bullfight in a barn, with our hair and beards grown long and full of loose reindeer hairs from the sleeping bags.

The procedure now adopted was for my party to pioneer the way. I was to drag only a light load, navigate, survey and select the camping sites. We were followed by the ponies, and the dogs brought up the rear.

We marched fifteen miles a day, and at the end of each march we constructed substantial snow walls to protect the ponies from the prevailing southerly wind.

The first pony, Jehu, was killed in latitude 81° 15', and two of our party turned northward and with two invalid dogs made their way back to the base. We in the advance party cut off great chunks of Jehu's flesh, which we put in the pemmican and ate with much relish, and the dogs, too, had a fine feed from the poor animal's carcase. The weather was fine generally, and the going easy.

Depots were established every sixty-five miles, and a week's provisions left in each for every returning sledge unit. We made excellent progress, and all went well until we had nearly reached latitude 84°.

Then we had the misfortune to encounter a blizzard of great severity, which blew for four days. This put back our chances of any great success it was the biggest knockdown blow that Scott had so far sustained in his expedition. Here he was, a day's march from the Beardmore Glacier, with fourteen men in fine health and high fettle, with dogs, ponies, food, and everything necessary for a great advance, but it was not to be. The blizzard prevented us getting on for five whole days, and during that time we had to be kept on full rations, for we were cold, wet through and hungry. Our tents quickly snowed up and there was nothing for us to do but eat and sleep whilst the blizzard pursued its course with unabated violence.

The temperature rose, however, and the falling snow turned first into driving sleet and then actual rain, which made the surface of the great ice barrier a sloppy morass. When the weather improved and we could march again, we had an awful day, for the ponies sank up to their bellies in the soft, wet snow and the men floundered in it thigh deep. In fifteen hours' marching we only covered five miles, and then we had to shoot all the ponies, as there was no food left for them. We made a big depot of their carcases and christened it Desolation Camp. For a couple of days after this the dog drivers accompanied us with their two teams. Then they gave us their sledge load of provisions, and themselves turned northwards.

We were now organized by our leader into three teams of four, each man pulling 170 pounds, and in this sledge formation we made the advance up the Beardmore Glacier, which is nearly 150 miles in length, and probably the biggest glacier in the world. Soft snow made dragging very heavy to begin with, and we made rather poor marches, but, as we climbed, the surface hardened, and on December 15, when we passed the eighty-fourth parallel of latitude, we began to stretch out our marches to the usual fifteen miles.

Halfway up the glacier we made a depot, and then, with lighter loads and better surfaces in our favour, we stretched our marches out to twenty miles a day. The great, glittering glacier was fringed with dark granite and dolerite hills. Some were snow-clad, and others almost bare, but it was a relief to have something to look at after the long journey over the great ice barrier. In latitude 85° we were nearly at the top of the glacier, and ahead of us was an overhang of ice falls and disturbances which made the road to the inland plateau look cruelly steep. On December 21, after a hard day's marching, we made our upper glacier depot 8,000 feet above the barrier level. There were a lot of crevasses, down which many of us slipped. Dr Atkinson and I both fell to the full length of our harness. It is a weird feeling to dangle in one of these bluey chasms, spinning round like a mouse hung in mid-air from the end of its own tail.

That night we said goodbye to the third supporting party – Dr Atkinson, Charles Wright, our distinguished Canadian chemist, Cherry-Garrard and Petty Officer Keohane. They left us next day, and when they reached the base station at Cape Evans they had covered eleven hundred and sixty-eight miles.

We must now follow the progress of the two remaining sledge teams, who were facing the last stage of the journey, the stretch from the summit of the Beardmore Glacier, over the King Edward VII plateau, to the Pole. Scott commanded one of the sledge teams and I had the other. We were dragging full loads of 190 pounds a man when we left the upper glacier depot and bade farewell to Atkinson's party. We steered south-westwards to begin with, to avoid the great ice fall which barred our way to the south. It took us three days to march round it. On Christmas Eve we made a splendid march over smooth, even, hard snow, and Christmas Day found us in high spirits, for we imagined

Members of Captain Scott's 'Terra Nova' Expedition team at Cape Evans in 1911.

that we were now clear of pressure ridges and crevasses. In this we were, however, disappointed. Late in the forenoon my sledge crossed a hidden crevasse; the snow bridge gave way, and Lashly, one of my party, whose forty-fourth birthday it was, celebrated it by dropping into a chasm to the full length of his trace.

We had great difficulty in rescuing Lashly, because our sledge just bridged this chasm, with only a few inches to spare at each end. Poor Lashly was spinning round some twenty feet below it, but we got him eventually to the surface by using our Alpine rope. Lashly was none the worse for his fall, and one of my party wished him a happy Christmas and another many happy returns of the day when he had regained safety. I will not repeat what Lashly said in reply.

That day we marched seventeen miles, and at the end of it we had the only full meal we really got on the great southern journey – extra biscuit, extra thick pemmican with pieces of pony meat in it, a chocolate and biscuit pouche, raisins, caramels, ginger, a double whack of cocoa and a great lump of butter each. Finally, Bowers, the stores officer, produced two little plum puddings. These he had secretly brought south, rolled up in a spare pair of socks.

The next few days our marches were splendid. We could drag on skis, and glided along at a good speed over the ice-capped plateau. It was very cold, though, and we constantly experienced a biting head wind which turned our breath to cakes of ice on our beards.

Scott had a double tent which kept him and his party warm, but we preferred to use a single tent and get more light and elbow room. Our food ration amounted to thirty-four ounces per man daily, and consisted of sixteen ounces of biscuit, which contained a high percentage of vegetable protein, twelve ounces of pemmican, and a small quantity of butter, eating chocolate, tea and cocoa. Occasionally we flavoured the pemmican with curry powder and, if the ration allowed, we sometimes put a handful of raisins in the pemmican. These raisins we all enjoyed.

Scott's tents, with bamboos and floor cloth complete, only weighed eighteen pounds, and I have never seen anything equal to them. They were most efficient and comfortable shelters, entirely his own invention. We used our sleeping bags as seats, the cooking was done in the centre of the tent, a small circular aperture which could be secured by stops formed the door, and the whole tent was anchored securely by big blocks of snow piled on the vallance.

We established the last depot of provisions on New Year's Eve in latitude 87°, and named it the 'Three Degree Depot', and on New Year's Day 1912 we continued towards the Pole with lighter loads.

We were now nearly 10,000 feet above the great ice barrier. The temperature was twenty degrees below zero, and a biting wind blew from the south. We had a hundred and eighty degrees of variation this day; that is to say, the north end of a compass needle pointed due south.

We were only pulling 130 pounds per man and we should have got along quite easily, but the height, the penetrating cold and the long marches now began to tell on us, and all of our party were weakening. We were thin and not nearly so full of energy as when travelling on the barrier.

On January 3, Captain Scott came into my tent and, sending my companions away, told me that he was taking his own team to the Pole. He asked me if I could spare one of my men and make the return journey of 750 miles shorthanded. He said he was quite sure of reaching the Pole, but not at all sure of getting back in the closing season with his party obviously weakening. Naturally I consented to spare one of my men, and Lieutenant Bowers, of the Indian Marine, left us to join the Polar party.

We could not all go to the Pole – there was not enough food for this. It was a disappointment, but not too great to bear. It would have been a far greater blow if we had known that Amundsen's tracks were almost in sight, and that the great Norwegian had got to the South Pole before us.

The next day we took four days' provisions, enough to get us back to latitude 87°, and handed over the rest of our load to Scott. We accompanied him for a few miles, and then, when we saw that his party was travelling rapidly and easily, we halted, shook hands all round and said goodbye. We gave three hearty cheers for the southern party, and they stepped off. We turned our sledge and commenced our long homeward march of over 750 miles. We frequently looked back until we saw the last of Captain Scott and his four companions – tiny black specks on a great white horizon of ice. Little did we think that we should be the last to see them alive, and that our three cheers on that bleak and lonely plateau summit would be the only appreciation they would ever know.

I am now going to ask you to forgive my talking a little about myself, but I must do this to tell you the story of the last supporting party.

After the first day's homeward march I realized that giving up one companion meant a good deal of extra marching, for if we were to remain on full provisions we had to average daily marches of seventeen miles until we got to the foot of the Beardmore. Day after day we fought our way northward over that featureless waste of snow, but we had two or three blizzard days which made it difficult to keep our course. We were muffled up tightly in our windproof clothing, and did all in our power to struggle along and keep a northward direction. The blizzard blinded and baffled us; it forced us always to turn our faces from it, and the stinging wind cut and slashed our cheeks like the constant jab of a thousand frozen needle points. Nevertheless, it was our party, the last supporting party, that Providence befriended. Whenever good luck was needed, we got it, and whenever poor Scott and his companions wanted fortune to smile, she only frowned upon them.

After three days we found ourselves right on the top of the Shackleton Ice Falls and gazed down upon the irregular surface of the Beardmore Glacier, hundreds of feet below us.

There were two ways in which we could reach the glacier: we could either march right round the Ice Falls as we had done coming south, which would waste three whole days; or we could take our lives in our hands and attempt to get the sledge slap over the falls.

We decided to take this risk and, with an acute sinking feeling in our hearts, the descent of the great Ice Falls was begun. We packed our skis on the sledge, attached spike rampants to our fur boots, and guided the sledge through a maze of hummocks and crevasses. We practically tobogganed down fifteen hundred feet, and narrowly escaped the crevasses, which frequently crossed our path. The speed of the sledge at one point must have been sixty miles an hour when we glissaded down a steep blue ice slope. I do not know how we escaped, as we did, entirely uninjured, and we reached the foot of the Ice Falls in a very short time and found that, by taking this hazard, we had saved nearly three days' marching and that much surplus food.

We had wonderful weather and sunshine for the next few days, and were in high glee at our progress. On the evening of January 16 we camped amongst rough ice and pressure ridges, expecting to reach the mid-glacier depot under the Cloudmaker Mountain next day. However, this was not to be, for a low, stratus cloud spread during the night like a tablecloth over the Beardmore and filled up its valley with mist. It was impossible to pick a good way down, and we got into awful trouble, and took two days to get clear. In some places we literally carried our sledge, which weighed nearly 400 pounds; in others we had to move gingerly across ice bridges flanked by inky blue chasms on both sides.

On January 17 and 18 we made eighteen-hour marches, hauling and humping our sledge over terribly rough ice, and when we reached the mid-glacier depot we were almost too exhausted to speak. The march down the lower part of the glacier brought no very exciting incident, beyond severe attacks of snow blindness, and we made very good progress.

But shortly after reaching the great ice barrier I was found to be suffering from scurvy. Day after day my condition became worse, until one day I fainted, and then I ordered my two companions to leave me in my sleeping bag, with what food they could spare, and to push on to safety. We could see the summit of the great snow-capped volcano, Mount Erebus, to the northward, so I knew that Crean and Lashly could now find their way home. It was here that we had the only act of insubordination in the expedition. The two men refused to leave me; they put me in my sleeping bag, strapped me on the sledge, and then for several days they dragged me northward until we reached the camp, where the motor sledges had been abandoned.

We spent the night here in our lonely little tent, but a new fall of snow entirely spoilt the surface, and when camp was struck next day the two men were quite unable to move the sledge. Their strength was spent after marching nearly 1,500 miles and, after one or two vain attempts, they realized that they could not drag me any further. They still refused to leave me, however, and re-erected the tent and put me in it in my sleeping bag. And then these two gallant fellows held a council.

It was thirty-five miles to Hut Point, where some assistance might possibly be obtained, and it was decided that Crean, who had not started dragging a sledge until we got to the Beardmore Glacier, should be the fitter man of the

Edward Evans with a sledging theodolite.

two. He therefore bade us goodbye and, taking with him practically all our remaining food, he started on that thirty-five-mile trudge across a badly crevassed area to Hut Point. It was a splendid effort on his part. He did the distance in eighteen hours, and collapsed on the floor of the little hut in the arms of Dr Atkinson and Dimitri, our dog driver, who were there with the two dog teams, replenishing the hut with supplies from Cape Evans.

Here again our astounding good fortune favoured us. When Crean had recovered somewhat he indicated our whereabouts; the dog teams were galloped out and our lives were saved. The King awarded the Albert Medal to both Crean and Lashly for their gallantry in helping me win through. It must be remembered that it was equally brave of Lashly to stay with me and nurse me until the end came, for without food and with only a little tea he could never have marched in later. Long sledge journeys in the Antarctic are fraught with danger and hazard; a long blizzard eats into the meagre food supply and sickness or accident to a companion means delay, which in turn may mean disaster and death.

Now turn your thoughts to Captain Scott and his four companions, whom we left marching southwards 144 miles from the Pole.

Soon after we had said goodbye, Scott came across the tracks of the Norwegian expedition. There were sledge tracks, ski tracks and dog tracks, many of them, and his party followed them to the Polar area. It was a great disappointment to find that Ronald Amundsen, the valiant Norseman, had forestalled them. Scott and his companions reached the South Pole on January 17, 1912, on a bleak and horrible day, with a hard wind blowing and the thermometer many degrees below zero. They found Amundsen's tent there with the Norwegian flag fluttering above it, and in the tent was a note telling them that Amundsen had reached the Pole just a month before.

Two days later Scott and his party began their return journey, with a distance of over nine hundred miles to cover. They made quite good marches to begin with, and went back at a fine pace over the ice-capped plateau; but the biting cold and hard winds caused them a good deal of frostbite, and Petty Officer Evans, who up till then had been considered the strongest man in the party, began to show signs of failing.

The little company got into very rough ice near the head of the Beardmore Glacier, and although they avoided the hazard of tobogganing down the Shackleton Ice Falls as we had done and used up valuable time in marching round them, they fell about a good deal and poor Evans struck his head on the hard blue ice and sustained a severe concussion.

From this day forward he caused Scott the greatest anxiety. He seemed to lose all confidence in himself and could not keep up with the team. The outlook became most serious. Bad weather was again encountered, and on February 17, near the foot of the Beardmore Glacier, poor seaman Evans died. Dr Wilson, Scott's trusted friend and companion in this great journey, said that Evans must have injured his brain by his fall. He was buried near Desolation Camp, where we had killed the last of our ponies on the outward march.

Evans was a splendid seaman and our sledge master; we owed to him the perfect fitting of our travelling equipment, every bit of which came under his charge. When they had buried him the little band pushed northward with great perseverance, although they must have known by their gradually shortening marches that there was little hope of reaching the winter quarters. Their best march on the great Ice Barrier was only twelve miles, and during the latter stages they dropped to only four miles in one day. This was not nearly good enough, for they had to average about fifteen to remain on full provisions.

Captain Oates, the only soldier in our expedition, was the next to go under. His feet and hands were dreadfully frost-bitten, and he constantly appealed to his companions for advice. They could only answer, 'Slog on, just slog on.' But Oates realized that the only hope of salvation for the party lay in his self-sacrifice, and on March 17, which was his birthday, he deliberately walked out to his death during a blizzard in a noble endeavour to save his three companions.

Captain Scott wrote in his diary: 'It was the act of a brave man and an English gentleman. We all hope to meet the end with a similar spirit, and assuredly the end is not far.' Scott, Wilson and Bowers fought their way on for another four days, without covering twenty miles in this time, and then they were forced by a blizzard to camp. The blizzard lasted for nine days. Their last camp was only eleven miles from the big depot at One Ton Camp, where there was food for six weeks. Eight months later their little tent was found, snowed under by the winter's storms.

Of the great Polar leaders, Nansen, Peary, Scott, Shackleton and Amundsen, have all comparatively recently crossed that silent, trackless ocean that leads to the explorers' Valhalla, all of them have set an example symbolical of the words carved on the memorial cross which overlooks the great Ice Barrier and Scott's last resting place. They are chosen from Tennyson's 'Ulysses':

'To strive, to seek, to find and not to yield.'

II

COURTING DISASTER IN
MYSTERY SHIPS

By REAR-ADMIRAL GORDON CAMPBELL, VC, DSO, MP

CAMPBELL, REAR-ADMIRAL GORDON. Born 1886; son of the late Colonel Frederick Campbell, CB, VD, and grandson of the late Sir John Campbell, Bart. Educated at Dulwich College and joined the Navy as a cadet in 1900. Served in Channel, Mediterranean and Pacific squadrons as a midshipman. Promoted Sub-Lieutenant, 1905; Lieutenant, 1907; served in the Flagship, China Squadron.

Appointed command of HMS *Ranger*, 1912; HMS *Bittern*, 1913

Appointed command of HMS *Q5* in October 1915. Promoted Lieutenant-Commander, October, 1915; Commander, 1916; awarded DSO, March 1916; bars to ditto, June 1917, August 1917; Captain, 1917; awarded VC, February 1917. Officiér Legion d'Honneur and awarded Croix de Guerre, avec palmes.

Commanded HMS *Active* and Patrol light cruisers, 1919–20. Commanded HMS *Impregnable* boys' training ship, 1921–22. Captain-in-Charge and Superintendent HM Dockyard, Simonstown, South Africa, 1923–25. Commanded HMS *Tiger*, 1925–27. Appointed ADC to HM the King in 1927. Promoted Rear Admiral, April 1928, and retired. Stood as candidate for Burnley, October 1931, and elected.

COURTING DISASTER IN MYSTERY SHIPS

'SOS. HAVE BEEN TORPEDOED.' THIS was the message that was daily being received from merchant ships during the Great War. It meant that another ship had fallen a victim to one of the enemy submarines: the blighters were all over the place, and as they had the great power of invisibility they were able to move about under water without being seen. The danger this country was then in, even now is not fully realized, for if the submarines had succeeded in cutting off our food supplies we should have lost the war. Luckily we had men like Jellicoe who realized and faced the danger.

A lot of different methods were employed to try to catch these fellows, but here I am just going to spin you a yarn about the Mystery or Q Ships, and in order to give you first-hand facts I will confine myself to the ones which I had the great honour to command. These Mystery Ships were merchant ships. At least they *looked* like merchant ships, but inwardly and concealed were naval guns and a naval trained crew. The first ship we fitted out was called *Farnborough*, or *Q5*. The crew had to dress up in plain clothes to be in keeping with the outward appearance of the ship. For this purpose the Admiralty, with their usual generosity, allowed each officer thirty bob and each man fifteen bob to supply himself with an outfit. By the time we were all dressed up we were a real motley crowd of toughs, in bowler hats or caps, and so on.

When we had got all the guns on board we went to sea to rehearse what we would do if we met a submarine. Our plan was this – and we aimed at the most highly organized efficiency and discipline. If a submarine attacked us, some of the crew were to rush for the boats, turn them out, lower them and then pull away from the ship as though abandoning it. In reality, of course, a party of men would still be left on board concealed at the guns. This 'Abandon Ship' was nicknamed 'Panic Party', and as it was usual then for masters of merchant ships to keep pets on board we arranged for the officer who went away in charge of the panic party to take with him a stuffed parrot in a parrot cage.

The object of all this was, of course, to hoax the submarine. It would see through its periscope the panic party taking to the boats, and would think that the ship was abandoned. It might then come to the surface of the water to take the Master prisoner or to obtain some fresh provisions, and we would at once cast off our disguise and destroy the submarine by gunfire.

Our first action was, as a matter of fact, comparatively simple compared with what was to follow. Early one morning we sighted a submarine, which fired a torpedo at us. The torpedo missed us, and eventually the submarine came to the surface and attacked us by gunfire. This gave us the chance to reply, which we promptly did, and succeeded in destroying the submarine.

But as time went on the enemy got wise to these tricks, and by the early part of 1917 they became particularly wary in approaching a merchant ship. New methods had now to be thought of to decoy the submarine to the surface of the water. It could no longer be induced to come up if the torpedo it fired missed its mark; but it might come up if the torpedo hit.

I had a wonderful crew, and I decided that the best way to get the submarine on to the surface of the water was deliberately to get torpedoed first. I therefore gave orders to my officers that if they saw a torpedo approaching the ship they were to increase or decrease speed, whichever was necessary to ensure its hitting. This was a great hazard, as we all knew that if the torpedo hit us in an unlucky place, such as the magazine or under the bridge, the whole lot of us would be blown to smithereens. But my staunch crew relished the idea

Gordon Campbell on deck with canine comrade.

of the adventure, and we went to sea on February 1, 1917, with the deliberate idea of getting torpedoed.

We had many days to wait, but as ships were being torpedoed all around us we knew it was only a matter of patience before our turn came, and sure enough on February 17 soon after breakfast we saw a torpedo approaching us from a long way off. One simple word of command, one slight alteration of helm and we could have avoided it – it was, of course, the natural instinct to try to avoid a torpedo – but we had decided on our course of action, and we deliberately allowed it to hit us. It got us on the engine-room bulkhead and exploded.

The panic party at once filled and lowered the boats and pulled away from the ship. Whilst this was going on, we who remained hidden on board could see the periscope of the submarine carefully watching every movement, so that we had to lay absolutely still.

This was no small ordeal, for the stern of the ship had quickly sunk to nearly water level, so that the men at the stern gun had water gradually creeping up to them. The engine room was soon flooded and the chief engineer and his firemen had to hide on top of the gratings as best they could. The wireless operator was cooped up in his tiny little room below decks. He knew that the ship had been torpedoed, and was sinking, but he had to remain still, as if nothing had happened. A few men were on the bridge with me, and others were concealed at the various guns. But to all intents and purposes the ship was abandoned, for not a soul aboard was visible to the enemy.

The submarine, still with only its periscope out of the water, came slowly and cautiously along. First it inspected the boats and then came alongside the ship. The strain for us on board was intense. The ship was sinking, yet we all had to lay absolutely motionless whilst the submarine subjected us to the most minute inspection.

It then steamed away, still submerged, as if about to leave us to our fate; but when it was some four hundred yards ahead of us the captain changed his mind and decided to come back for prisoners and fresh provisions. This was his undoing. The submarine came right on to the surface of the water and steamed round and back. When she was abreast of my bridge, about a hundred yards off, I gave the order to 'open fire'. The White Ensign was hoisted at the masthead, down fell the sides with a clatter and in a few seconds the guns were hurling shot and shell at the bewildered submarine.

There is no need to dwell on the destruction. It was a short affair, and in a few minutes the submarine had sunk beneath the waves for the last time. Some of the crew were seen struggling in the water, and our boats were able to save two of them.

We now had to send out a message for assistance, and our ship was taken in tow by a sloop. After many mishaps she was eventually beached on the south coast of Ireland, with her stern eight foot under water and a list of nearly forty degrees.

The crew had been through a very stiff test of discipline and they endured it without a flinch. I think this was the first case of a ship destroying a submarine after being torpedoed, and there was only one more case, which I will tell you about now.

I suggested to the crew that we should fit out another ship and try the same tactics again, and they were all for it. The fitting out took nearly two months, and we sailed again at the end of May under the name of *Pargust*.

This time we did not have so long to wait for a torpedo. On our seventh day out, again at breakfast time, we saw one coming straight at us, and it got us bang in the engine room. By an extraordinary chance it only killed one man; the other man in the engine room was blown on to the upper deck and survived. The engine room was instantly flooded, whilst the panic party were busy getting away in the boats. We didn't have such good cover in this ship and one of the gun crews had to lay prone on the deck, in fact they had to pretend they were part of the deck.

You can imagine the strain. They knew the ship was filling with water, yet if they made the slightest movement it would be spotted by the submarine which was cruising watchfully around us. It was forty minutes after we had been hit when the submarine at last came right up and made for the boat with the supposed Master in it. It seemed like forty hours. But we bided our time, and as he came abreast the ship the White Ensign was hoisted, down clattered the ship's sides and off went the guns. The crew of the submarine came tumbling out of the hatch and held up their hands in surrender, and we at once ceased fire; but no sooner had we done so than the submarine began to steam off into the mist. There was no alternative now but to open fire again, and in a few minutes we had destroyed it. Then we got help for our own ship and towed her 400 miles to Plymouth, where we left her.

We had now made a bag of three submarines, the greatest number made by any one crew, and the King honoured us by awarding the ship the Victoria Cross, which was to be balloted for and worn by one officer and one man. This meant

Depiction of The Royal Navy Q-ship HMS Dunraven *in combat with the German U-Boat – 8th August 1917.*

that he considered all officers and men were equally deserving. The officer who received it was the First Lieutenant, now Captain Stuart of the C.P.R. line, and the man was Seaman W. Williams of Holyhead.

The crew all volunteered to go on with the job, but some of them were showing signs of nerves and had to be left behind. After all it isn't everybody who can stand being torpedoed more than a couple of times.

We now fitted out a beautiful ship called the *Dunraven* with all the latest devices we could think of, for the enemy was becoming more and more wily. We had iron plates put round the bridge as a protection against splinters, since the submarines carried large guns now, which they generally used. We had a steam pipe with a lot of holes in it laid round the centre of the ship, so that by opening a valve on the bridge a cloud of steam could be sent up from the middle of the ship to make the enemy think that we had been hit in the engine room. Then, so as to appear to be carrying a real cargo, we had some full-sized railway trucks constructed of canvas and wood, which was quite a novel idea. In the poop or stern of the ship were four depth charges, each containing 300 lbs. of TNT There were also two magazines full of ammunition. On top of the poop, carefully concealed, was a big gun with the gun crew under the command of Lieutenant Bonner.

As soon as the fitting out was completed we sailed for the Bay of Biscay, where we knew a submarine was operating. On our fourth day out, about seven bells – that is to say eleven-thirty o'clock in the forenoon – we sighted her on our starboard side. She rapidly submerged and we just steamed on as if we hadn't noticed her – but we knew all the time that this invisible boat was going to attack us. This period of waiting to be attacked by an invisible enemy is a particularly trying one and tests one's nerves and coolness to the extreme. On this occasion it lasted half an hour, and then the submarine appeared directly astern of us, some 5,000 yards away, and opened fire with her big gun. This was too big a range for us to chance, so we acted our part of merchant ship and returned the fire with a little gun we carried in the stern.

All merchant ships carried one of these, which was commonly referred to as a defensive gun. The crew of this gun had strict orders to make their shots fall short so as to entice the submarine closer. At the same time we emitted a lot of black smoke from the funnel to pretend we were trying to escape, but in reality we reduced speed by a knot.

The submarine continued to shell us for a solid hour, but none of her shots actually hit us. They were all falling just ahead of us so that we were steaming into the spray of the explosions all the time. At length she ceased fire and closed in to about 1,000 yards; but this was still too big a range for us to risk, so we let the fellow shell us again. The shots were now falling all around us and it was obvious that we were going to be hit at any minute. We naturally didn't relish the idea of getting plugged in the magazine or someplace which would disclose our real identity, so I decided to make use of our steam pipe and warned the crew to be ready for 'Panic Party'.

A few minutes later a shell exploded alongside the engine room. Now was the time. The valve was opened and a cloud of steam gushed up from the middle of the ship. At the same time the panic party took to the boats as if we had at last abandoned hope of escape.

The submarine must have seen the cloud of steam, but whether it saw the panic party I do not know. Anyhow it didn't take the hint, but continued to fire, and an unlucky shot hit us in the poop and blew Bonner out of his place of concealment. With great presence of mind, however, he crawled into the gun hatch with the remainder of his gun crew.

An able seaman named Morrison, who was in charge of the depth charges, was also blown through the poop doors and was badly wounded; but with great gallantry, which cost him his life, he crawled back to his place of duty without giving the show away.

Two more shells followed into the poop and set the whole place on fire. This satisfied the submarine, which now stopped firing and steamed towards us. But unfortunately such volumes of black smoke were now pouring out of the poop that it was practically impossible to see the submarine, so I decided to hold fire till it got clear of the smoke.

These were indeed moments of intense strain. The fire in the poop was raging round the magazine, and lying concealed just above this fire were Bonner and his gun crew. At any second, I knew, the magazine would explode, and they would be blown up, and they knew it too.

Bonner tried to communicate with me by the voice pipe, but he couldn't do so as it had been shot away. So entirely on their own initiative Bonner and his crew decided to sit tight where they were, knowing perfectly well that they were going to be blown up. Could anything be braver? They could of course have left their gun and come out on deck, but as the ship was supposed to be abandoned it might have spoilt the whole show. They realized this and decided to sacrifice their lives sooner than give the game away.

Just as the submarine was coming clear of the smoke the explosion occurred. All the depth charges blew up and the gun crew and gun complete were hurled into the air. As luck would have it, however, they landed on the railway trucks, which broke their fall before they reached the iron deck, and although they were all seriously wounded, chiefly in the head or legs, they all survived the action. The submarine of course now knew what we were and dived under water as hard as it could.

We were now in rather a predicament. Our ship was on fire and we were also shortly going to be torpedoed. The choice before us was either to get the panic party on board and make a dash for harbour or else to have another go at the submarine. We decided on the latter course, and a signal was made to all ships to keep away. We then transferred the

HMS Dunraven *under fire.*

wounded to the saloon and waited to get torpedoed. There would be no chance of the torpedo missing us, for the ship was stopped and flames were spurting from the poop – but the crew remained quite calm, though I must admit it was an uncanny situation.

At last, after what seemed an eternity, but was in reality only half an hour, we saw the torpedo coming. It got us in the hold, which happened to be stacked with wood, so no one was hurt, but it unfortunately cracked the engine-room bulkhead and allowed water to enter there.

We now did a second 'Abandon Ship'; the boats were recalled and an additional party of men put into them; we also launched a raft, to pretend that the last man had now really left the ship. This left us with only two guns' crews instead of five to fight the submarine.

When the boats had got clear of the ship the submarine came along with its periscope out of the water and steamed round and round us and in and out of the boats. It continued this for over an hour and our ammunition in the poop was exploding all the time, whilst my two guns' crews remained motionless.

Eventually the poop got burnt out and the submarine came up directly astern of the ship about 100 yards away and proceeded to shell us again with its big gun.

We couldn't return the fire as our stern gun was gone, and we couldn't steam round and get the enemy that way as we had no steam to steam round with, so we just had to grin and bear it – a very unpleasant business, since we could actually see the Germans loading and pointing their gun at us. The shells made a nasty mess of the bridge and but for the iron plate I shouldn't be alive now.

This went on for twenty minutes, and then the submarine submerged again and came along to have another look at us. I decided to have a go at the blighter with our torpedoes, but the hull of the submarine was too deep for them to travel down to it properly. Our first torpedo passed over the top of it and the second hit it without exploding. The submarine heard it hit. This, of course, gave the game away and the submarine submerged once more.

There seemed little to hope for us now. No doubt we should get torpedoed till we sank; but I hurriedly arranged for a third 'Abandon Ship' when the next torpedo came, intending to try and see the U-boat out with one gun crew.

However, the chance never came. We learnt afterwards that it had no more torpedoes to attack us with, but in any case an American patrol yacht arrived on the scene just then and chased the submarine away.

We had been in action nearly five hours and it was a

terrible disappointment not to get our foe. Anyhow it had been a fair and square fight and we had lost; my crew had behaved magnificently, and if any mistake was made the responsibility was mine alone.

We now had to try to save the *Dunraven*. The wounded and all but twenty of my crew were transferred to another ship and the destroyer *Christopher* got us in tow. We lasted some time, thanks to our cargo of wood. At about 2 a.m., with half a gale blowing, the water was up to the bridge, so I told the destroyer to send a boat to take us off and ordered my twenty men to fall in on the foredeck.

I joined them there, and found them standing in dead silence. I warned them that the boat would only hold four men; any more might capsize it.

Not a man moved. Then the senior one said to me, 'Will you please mention four men by name, as the boat will only have time for one trip before the ship sinks?' So I had to mention four men by name and that was the only trip the boat did.

We were now standing in water and had to fall in again on the forecastle head. But the destroyer managed to get the rest of us off. With very fine seamanship he bumped his bows against ours and one by one the crew jumped from the deck of the *Dunraven* on to the deck of the destroyer. But no man jumped till I personally told him to do so.

By the time the last of us went the *Dunraven* had sunk in a vertical position. I was very proud to have witnessed the closing scenes of this ship, though much the same as those of many others. Discipline and unselfishness were maintained to the end.

The King awarded the Victoria Cross to Lieutenant Bonner and also to his crew. This was balloted for, the ballot falling on Petty Officer Pitcher, the captain of the gun. The remainder of the gun's crew received the Conspicuous Gallantry Medal, and a posthumous one was also awarded to the late Seaman Morrison.

When he made these and other awards the King stated in his own hand that he considered that 'greater bravery than was shown by all officers and men on this occasion could hardly be conceived.'

III

IN THE DEPTH OF THE SEA

By KAPITÄN A. D. ERNST HASHAGAN

HASHAGAN, KAPITÄN ERNEST. Was posted to the Imperial German Navy as an officer in 1905, and employed throughout the War in submarines. When Commander of the *U62* he sunk the mystery ship *Q 12*.

IN THE DEPTH OF THE SEA

ADMIRAL GORDON CAMPBELL WAS, AS you know, commander of your Q or Mystery Ships. That was an extremely risky job; but no doubt it occurred to you that there was another side to that story – our side. As soon as we U-boat commanders realized – after sad experience – that things were not always what they seemed, and that the harmless-looking old tramp steamer might really be concealing such unpleasant people as your Admiral Gordon Campbell, the war between Q-boats and U-boats became a real duel of wits.

I do not know whether I ever had the honour of crossing the inviting path of Admiral Campbell. Perhaps I did once inspect through my periscope, from a polite distance, the rusty sides and slovenly gear of his 'harmless' old hulk, laden down to the Plimsoll line and rashly proceeding on her way as though she had never heard of the war. Perhaps some inner voice of warning spoke in time, and I decided that the sheep's clothing was perhaps a little too sheepish, or not sheepish enough, and that discretion was the better part of valour. At any rate, we never left cards on each other, for if we had it is very probable that you would not have heard both our stories in this series. But if I didn't meet Admiral

Campbell, I met some of his confederates.

On April 30, 1917, I was cruising in fine weather on the western approaches of Ireland. A faint patch of smoke hung over the southern horizon; two masts as fine as needle-points appeared, and then suddenly a funnel and smoke again. We dived and made our way towards the unknown ship. In half an hour we could already see something more.

A black steamer reeling along like a drunken man, steering a wild, zigzag course. We approached nearer and nearer. She was altering her course every ten minutes, and each time by about fifteen degrees. Why? We counted and calculated, puzzled and guessed the reason for her zigzag system and figured out a mean course for ourselves to cross hers before she passed. This flying a common, rather tattered, red ensign was remarkable, I thought.

The British don't use that as a rule. In fact, there is a vague something in the air that calls for caution. The coxswain beside me has his hand on the lever of the periscope motor, following my orders.

'Run in the periscope! In: deeper yet! Out a shade. In, in!'

So the eye is always under water, only coming clear of the spray for fractions of a second. The enemy is fast altering course again; I see her pause as if trying to make up her mind; then she comes straight towards us. still as death in my boat. Only the rattle of the hydroplanes and the laconic orders for the periscope. And then the vessel's bows swim into the periscope's field. It is as still as death in my boat. Only the rattle of the hydroplanes and the laconic orders for the periscope. And then the vessel's bows swim into periscope view.

'First tube, stand by!'

'First tube, shoot!'

There is a slight shiver forward in the boat. The torpedo has gone. It is a dead shot. I feel it. Twenty seconds pass and then come two heavy detonations with violent shocks to us in the boat. We retire to ten fathoms, come to periscope depth again and look round. The ship is heavily buckled amidships. There is no sign of the crew. Then, as I cross her bows with my periscope well out – a decoy manoeuvre – a heavy fire is opened on us from a concealed gun under the bridge. So my suspicions are confirmed, for I also see now another very well-masked heavy gun in the stern. The concealing flaps have been splintered and pushed aside by the explosion of the torpedo. There is no doubt any longer what sort of ship we have disposed of. It is the submarine decoy, Q 12.

The end of Q 12 was short. The game was up and the crew took to the boats. The panic party did not come properly into action. The stage of the play appeared to be sinking. At a safe distance we surfaced, and I photographed the wreck from three fathoms below the surface. Then we set about it with two powerful guns. It split right in two amidships and went down in separate parts amidst a cloud of smoke and flame. I took its commander, Commander Lewis, a prisoner, and left his men to be picked up by some passing vessel. But our main task was not, of course, to do battle with these Q boats, but to prowl about and sink merchant ships with valuable cargoes.

In August 1917, I worked at the entrance of the St. George's Channel. The breeze was strong and the sea heavy. Early in the morning we attacked a steamship. The torpedo track was visible under the target, but no explosion followed. I entered in my log: unexplained misfire. We surfaced, but after a few minutes' fresh air we were attacked by an aeroplane and dived again. It notified its arrival with a load of bombs. Luckily for us there was a few feet of water between us and the bombs, but the force of the explosion upset my boat to such an extent that the bows came right out and the whole conning tower broke surface like the dorsal fin of a shark. But our luck was in. The airman had dropped all his bombs already and had nothing solid enough handy for this lovely target.

Towards dawn we were feeling our way to the much-used steamship track between the Kish Lightship and Holyhead. We could not complain of boredom, since the sea around us was alive with destroyers, patrols and steamships. A big, deep-laden ship was our objective. She seemed to be making for Liverpool; but she was escorted by two destroyers and it was obviously a difficult matter to get at her.

In the pitch darkness we had already got too close to one of the destroyers and evidently some of the oily smell from our Diesel exhausts had reached her nostrils. At all events, both destroyers became greatly excited.

Then there suddenly appeared a bright light to starboard, astern. My hand flew by instinct to the alarm gong, but hesitated a moment. What was it? Had they seen us? Were we in urgent danger? We watched; then through the night flashed the abrupt Morse signal: 'Keep a sharp look-out. German submarine ahead!' One destroyer is warning the other over our heads! A ray of the enemy's searchlight hovers uncertainly on our bridge. My men laugh. They'll never see us, Captain!

I decided to hold out a few seconds longer. Like a wraith, the slim outline of the second destroyer passes by and fades into the darkness. Behind it, a much larger shape looms out of the night – the steamship! We have broken through the escort and now our way is clear.

Our torpedo takes the ship in the forehold. We stand by, watching, a few hundred yards away. But what is this? The shadow of the vessel grows larger, grows gigantic. Is she still making headway then? She comes at us like a bull, head down. She is doomed.

Until our oil fuel was almost at an end we worked in this way. Then we had to think about making for home.

There were two ways back. Up northwards, round the Orkneys, one door to Germany stood wide open. The patrols might annoy us a little; but we should probably get through all right. To southward there was also a door – the Straits of Dover – but it was locked and barred against submarines by the British barrage, that long, submerged, steel net, suspended from buoys, crossing and recrossing from Dover to Calais. There were mines in front of the net and behind it. There were mines even in the nets themselves fastened on in such a way as to go off if any heavy foreign body bumped in anywhere and excited a pull. There were also sunken blockships for the submarine to ram herself against when she was trying to get through the nets. We didn't know exactly how this barrage system looked beneath the surface; but we had been able to construct a diagram which wasn't, in fact, far from the truth.

The depth of the water between Dover and Calais varied from 12 to 20 fathoms. It only attained a depth of 26 fathoms in one place, and this place was called the deep-water channel. We assumed that the nets would not hang right down to the sea bottom at this point and that a submarine which had failed to slide unseen over the barrage on the surface, through the floats and buoys, on a dark or misty night, would be able to dive right under it through this deep-water channel. Should we go by the Orkneys or risk the barrage?

There would be more likelihood of doing successful work *en route* this second way and I reckoned up on my fingers that it would take us two days to get to the western entrance of the Channel, and we could put in four day's work by Cape Lizard or Start Point before we made the run through the barrage.

I glanced at the calendar. Full moon! There it stood, inexorable. So to get over the barrage on the surface might be extremely difficult – the more so if it was calm and clear; but then the weather lately had been stormy and misty, and we stood a good chance of being sheltered by dark clouds.

We decided to take the risk. If we failed to surface the barrage we would dive for the deep-water channel.

By the evening of August 31 we had done our work and arrived at the Colbert Bank Lightship. What was the weather going to be like for getting through? We knew soon enough.

A reddish light shone out behind the French coast which lay clearly visible in the calm night. It was the moon which mounted swiftly, red and gigantic into the sky. Never have I seen such a moon! Its ugly face hung, with a mocking grin, above us and the battlefields of the Western Front.

'Come on, you Germans; come along! I'll light you home all right, so that you'll never forget this night,' it seemed to say.

On the bridge we looked at one another. This 'face' was grotesque, uncanny. It turned night into day. A clear cloudless sky, quiet sea, sharp horizon and the great monstrous arc-lamp in the heavens. Well, never mind; we may get over the barrage unseen yet with a bit of luck.

German U-boat on patrol in the Atlantic.

German U-boat cruising in the Mediterranean – April 1917.

'Both engines full speed ahead!'

We proceed unmolested on the surface as far as Boulogne. The lighthouses of Cape Gris Nez and Dungeness, greatly dimmed, shine across at us. Off Cape d'Alprecht we are confronted by a host of vessels and forced to dive.

Soon after midnight we surface again: all hands remain at the diving stations, and at high speed we make for the barrage, which is about ten miles off. Now or never!

Then, I observe in my powerful night glasses, a tiny dot to the northward on the moonlit sea. There is scarcely a second for thought. It is a submarine chaser! In less than half a minute the sea has closed smoothly above us and only just in time. The enemy shoots up, with a big bow wave.

'Look out! Depth charges coming,' I call down the voice pipe to the control room.

Already now their thunder is tearing the silence to pieces and making a maelstrom of the sea round the boat. All round us roar the bombs. The range is considerable, but we experience a most violent concussion in the boat. So the barrage patrols are already on the qui vive and a surface breakthrough is now impossible. We must take our last remaining chance; remain submerged and dive under the whole area of nets and mines, but we are still such a long way from the barrage that we shall have a great deal of difficulty now in finding our gap, the deep-water channel.

From now on the submarine chaser follows faithfully. He is hot on our trail. We can plainly hear his screws, above, behind and alongside us. No doubt Véry lights are mounting into the sky, searchlights playing, wireless sparking out:

'Hullo! Enemy submarine close in front of barrage steaming to the northward. Look out! Don't let her through. Catch the fish in the net. Bring her up alive or send her down dead, but don't let her through.'

We are all gathered in the control room, with the chart of the barrage before us. The giant hull of our boat is humming along close above the bottom. Every now and then it hits the bottom with a jerk that throws us off our feet. At ninety feet the pointer jumps and trembles. Still ninety feet? Surely it must get deeper soon. Or is the tide setting more strongly on to the French coast tonight, so that we should be keeping out more? We steer down again, always with the feeling that we must 'duck our heads' as low as possible to get under the nets. This time our impact with the bottom is unpleasantly severe. Eighty feet. Good God! it is getting shallower instead of deeper. How can that be possible?

Every sense works feverishly. In our mind's eye we see the net, wide stretched, hanging before us the gap must be to the left. Port, more to port. At that moment the starboard side of the boat scrapes heavily against some object on the bottom. There is a thunderous hammering as if great blocks of rock are rolling over us, the boat lists over heavily, rights herself, strikes bottom heavily again. Eighty feet still!

We must be close in front of the barrage now. 'Hard to port,' I yell to the helmsman and brace myself instinctively against some fearful power that would impose its will on us. Something quite out of the ordinary must happen now that alone can save us. My best helmsman, who is always at the helm when danger threatens, quietly turns his wheel as if he were standing in the sunshine. Degree by degree, the boat swings round the compass card. The tide is now pushing us broadside on towards the nets. But no matter. Either we find deep water within a very few minutes, or else we run straight into the deadly arms of the nets and mines.

Again the boat strikes bottom: 95 feet! A sigh of relief; 100 feet, 120 feet; at last, at last! Now we are in more than 130 feet. 'Hard a-starboard, steer 20.' The boat swings back to her old course. At the last minute, it seems, we have found the deep water. Now we are under the barrage. A loud explosion behind us: the stern gives a heave and the starboard propeller suddenly begins to turn irregularly. But otherwise all is still. Once again we hear propellor noises above us. And so we slip away.

Only when hours have gone by and all remains silent, we come nearer to the surface and take a look round. At daybreak we surface. We are alone and through!

On September 2 we run safely in Heligoland. One blade of our starboard propeller is heavily dented and split. The starboard after hydroplane is bent upwards. We must have fouled the net with our starboard side and taken a piece of it with us. It was that pull which exploded a charge some distance off, and merely knocked away some of our 'trimmings' without damaging us seriously.

We lay in the dock very well pleased with ourselves. Our 'whale' had had a sharp rap on his tail! But he had only given himself a good shake and come through.

IV

TWENTY-FOUR HOURS IN THE FOREIGN LEGION

By MAJOR P. C. WREN

WREN, MAJOR PERCIVAL CHRISTOPHER. He is descended from the well-known traveller, Christopher Wren, who lived in the reign of Charles I, and from Sir Christopher Wren. He has served in many armies, the British, French and Indian, and in five Continents. He has been soldier, sailor, journalist, educationalist, novelist and traveller. His most renowned book *Beau Geste* ran to over a million copies and was translated into the language of every country in the world.

TWENTY-FOUR HOURS IN THE FOREIGN LEGION

IN RECENT YEARS A GOOD many books have been published concerning that amazing military organization, the French Foreign Legion.

As a result, or perhaps a cause of this, a good deal of public interest has been aroused in the Legion, the more so, doubtless, by reason of the titles of these books, the majority of which call the Legion, 'Hell', and allude to its members as damned.

Probably the hand of the journalist rather than that of the genuine ex-legionnaire is responsible for the more lurid touches and purple patches. Anyhow, there has been a vast amount of nonsense, a great deal of rubbish, and much absolute untruth written on the subject.

It is noteworthy that three British officers who saw service in the Legion wrote books that were far from being sweeping condemnations of the famous Regiment. On the other hand, an officer who served with distinction throughout the Great War in a Royal Fusilier Regiment, and then throughout the Riff Campaign in the French Foreign Legion, concluded an account of his experiences with the words: 'Home at last after five years of Hell...'

But I am not concerned with the general subject of Life in the French Foreign Legion, so much as with one particular Hazard. I went to the *Bureau de Recrutement* in the Rue St. Dominique for enlistment in the Legion, and, to be quite fair and honest, I fully admit that the recruiting officer there made no secret of the fact that he thought I was a fool. I thought it was very decent of him. He didn't actually try to deter me from joining; but he mentioned casually that the Foreign Legion was rather the Spiritual Home of the labourer, the long-service professional soldier, and the man who had really roughed it in earnest. He added that he would be very glad to enlist me, in view of my inches and enthusiasm, but I must go away and sleep on it, think it over in the light of what he had said, and return next day if I were still of the same foolish mind.

I returned. I was vetted *bon pour le service* by the Medical Corps doctor, and enlisted. I had contracted to serve France for five years in any part of her colonial possessions for the sum of a halfpenny a day, without deductions or income tax.

Purely in the spirit of romance and make believe for I was not fleeing from Justice I took a name that was not my own. Most legionnaires do this. A few, because they are fugitive criminals and the vast majority for the same reason that small boys wear black masks or feather headdresses when playing robbers or Red Indians.

I travelled that night to Fort St. Jean at Marseilles, the bureau depôt and clearing house of the XIX Army Corps, which is the Army of Africa. Here, it is true, I found dirt, discomfort, fatigues, nasty menial, manual labour, and

French Legionnaire in the heat of the desert.

somewhat rough contemptuous treatment; but what did these things matter? My barracks was a moated mediaeval castle, within sight of Monte Cristo's Chateau d'If, and my companions were wearing the most romantic and attractive uniforms in the world!

Every branch and service of the French Army was represented, and if the noise were reminiscent of a parrot house, so were the colourfulness and the exotic sights and sounds. There were Spahis, in incredibly gorgeous dress, Zouaves, Turcos, Tirailleurs, Chasseurs d'Afrique, Colonial Infantry, Gunners, Sappers and Legionnaires: and undoubtedly the parrots could swear – as well as eat, drink and flutter gay plumage.

I was thrilled, and couldn't see or hear enough of these men who brought a breath of so strange and different a life from across the seamen who had marched and served and fought in such strange places – men from Africa! And I thought of a Latin tag from schoolboy days: 'There's always something new from Africa.'

I made no friends among the recruits on our way to join the Legion. Frankly, I didn't like the look of them. Nor did I gather that they particularly liked the look of me. They were mostly unshaven, unwashed, collarless men, rather rough, rather dirty, and with ways that differed widely from those to which I had been accustomed. They were entirely foreign to me in speech and habits, and some of them reminded me of the sea-captain's terse official report on the manners and customs of the Cannibal Islanders: 'Manners none and customs nasty!'

After a few days at Fort St Jean we were shipped across to Oran in Algeria, and taken thence by train eighty miles inland, to Sidi bel Abbès, the depôt of the 1st Battalion.

Here things were different. We had our uniforms now, and uniform was a great leveller. We were all soon shaved and clean and shining bright. Everyone understood French, which was the *lingua franca*, and one quickly found one's own level, and companions of one's own sort and kind. That is one of the marvels of the Legion. Every nation is represented and not only every class, but every sort and kind, every rank and trade and profession. I was most enthusiastic, and derived endless interest from observing my comrades – the most incredibly mixed assemblage of men on the face of the earth. They included not only people of all the nations of Europe, but even Chinese, Japanese, Arabs and assorted Africans.

I was glad when I completed a selection of representatives of all five continents by meeting an Australian and more than one American.

I have to tell you about one particular day of glorious life in the Legion, and will first describe some of the men of my own *escouade*, my comrades of the day in question.

First of all, there was Pierre. You would have liked Pierre – one of the merriest souls I ever met. Nothing could damp his joyous cheerfulness, except wine, and that in sufficient quantity to quench him altogether. Pierre only ceased to be amusing when he could speak no more. Only at one stage of his long and happy journeys from sobriety to speechlessness was he ever a bore, and that was the moment the inevitable moment – when he would tell you all about his murder. I am afraid the story must have been true, for he always told it in the same way and never varied a detail. And nothing could stop him.

'And to think how kind I always was to her,' he would expostulate. 'I hardly ever beat her when she didn't deserve it. She always had plenty to eat – when there was plenty; and she frequently tasted wine – when I was asleep… Why, I actually married the woman. And what did she do when my back was turned – and my stomach was being badly turned – while I was doing six months in The Box for borrowing money from a bourgeois, without telling him, one night, in the Place Pigalle? She went off with Tou-Tou-Boil-the-Cat, the lieutenant of our band. Fact. She did. She won't again, though. I went after her when I came out.

'"Your heart's in the right place, my love," I said. "It's your head that leads you astray." Then I cut it off. *Oui, Monsieur*. I, Pierre Pompom, held her up by her hair with my right hand – so – and cut her head off. *Psstt!* Yes. With this very knife.'

And at this point Pierre would produce a knife from the back of his belt.

Yes, I believe Pierre was a murderer. But he was a very nice one to meet, and only made these *faux pas* – or talked about them – when not quite himself. I never met a braver man in my life. He was true as steel, a splendid comrade, and faithful unto death.

In curious contrast to him was Müller, a German – an aristocrat, an ex-officer and a typical Junker. He was as self-controlled and unemotional as Pierre was vivacious and flamboyant.

'Hans Müller', he called himself (though he was certainly *von* and *zu* and probably *Graf* or *Baron*, and possibly Hohenzollern or Hohenlohe). He was a man who simply hated to laugh with joy, or swear with rage, or to express any emotion whatsoever. His exceedingly handsome face, with its cold blue eyes, high-bridged nose, golden moustache, hard mouth and fine chin, was a face that never changed – never smiled or frowned. And this wasn't by any means because he was stupid, stolid or phlegmatic: not a bit of it. He was an extremely clever man – musical, widely read, highly cultured, travelled, and, in the best sense of the word, a gentleman. I knew nothing of his life, but only of his death. Why he joined the Legion I don't know. But there was certainly a woman in his story. For in a quiet voice and with an expressionless face, he would speak most bitterly of women. And it was his intention to remain in the Foreign Legion until he died.

There was Ramon Diego, a very tough Spaniard from the Pyrenees, smuggler or smuggler's muleteer, known as 'The Devil'. And he was a devil to fight, though unfortunately he would only fight with a knife. As he explained, it was the weapon he had been taught to use in childhood, and since then he had used no other. He was a big, dark, saturnine, smouldering sort of volcano, always about to erupt. Much respected by those who didn't care for knife fighting.

I was very fond of Ramon, a simple forthright soul.

Then there was 'Ivan the Terrible' – six foot seven: I am not sure it wasn't six foot eight – weight unknown, as he always broke the machine. He had been a subaltern of the famous Preobrazhenski Regiment of the Imperial Guard (alas! no more, I fear), and made no secret of how he came to the Legion. He went on leave, and followed a lady, of whose appearance he approved, the length of the Siberian Railway from Port Arthur to St. Petersburg, thence to Paris, on to Marseilles and across to Algiers.

There the dream had ended, probably with Ivan's money. And finding the French Legion nearer than his Russian Regiment, and probably much more likely to extend a welcome, Ivan had turned in with them, instead of going back. He was a great lad with a heart of gold, a tongue of silver, a hand of iron, and a front of brass.

Torvaldsen the Dane was another fine fellow: so clean-looking and clean-living. A seeker of adventure.

Cortlandt, the Dutchman, unlike nearly all Dutchmen, was a bad lot, though he had had a lot to make him bad. And once he was up against a sergeant, his stubborn Dutch spirit kept him there. He used to drink a vile rice spirit called *tchum-tchum*, which was, I suppose, the nearest thing he could get to *Schnapps*, and when he had had a drink or two of this poison, he would seek me out and remind me that the Dutch once sailed up the Medway. I invariably replied: 'Never mind, Fatty. Nobody noticed them.' And he would go away and think this over, with the help of more *tchum-tchum*, until he fell asleep.

What makes the particular day I am going to tell you about an outstanding one for me, is the fact that on it I lost these friends of mine, and though I hadn't known them long I missed them badly; also because I got an interesting little souvenir scar on my head and an interesting little souvenir dagger which now decorates my study wall, having failed to decorate my stomach.

We were on the march, and in a hurry. We slept where we dined, and we dined where we fell down, after marching the whole of a terrible day, over sand. Although I had done some gruelling marches during training days and after, I thought of the warning of the recruiting officer in Paris. There was, as he had ironically said, 'Lots of sand; blue sky; no rain; no snow; no fog; sunshine – sunshine all the time.' Camels (glimpsed far off-with scouts on them), mirages, palms and oases (in the mirages). I thought not only of the recruiting officer, but of Coleridge's *Ancient Mariner* and his bitter complaint. You may know the verse beginning:

'And all in a hot and copper sky
The bloody sun at noon
Stood right above...'

...the whole beastly show. And at 4 a.m. next morning the buglers blew reveille, and this particular, slightly hazardous day in the Legion began.

I rolled over and dressed – by putting on my *képi*. I then slipped on my equipment, and was ready. I was particularly ready for my share of the contents of the pail brought from the company cooking fire by Ivan the Terrible. It was hot, liquid, sweet, and had an unmistakable flavour of coffee. I dipped out a mugful of this heartening brew, and produced the remainder of my breakfast from my haversack. If I remember rightly, it was a hard, dry biscuit and some soft, wet macaroni.

Depiction of French Foreign Legion in action from Beau Geste – *Lordprice Collection: Alamy Stock Photo.*

We fell in by sections, each section in three ranks, so that when we got the order to right turn and march, we marched in threes, and not in columns of fours as the British Army does. One long march is very like another, but this was more so than most, by reason of the record length, the record heat, the soft looseness of sand, and the fact that we were marching, by compass, across sand dunes, and were perpetually climbing up one side and down the other, instead of marching on the flat.

We were literally crossing an uncharted ocean – of sand; and its billows were as regular, numerous and monotonous as those of any of the great ocean wastes of waters. However, we realized that it was necessary to avoid the usual road or caravan route, for we were hastening to the relief of a suddenly beleaguered fort; and the Arabs would no doubt be on the watch for us on the road. We were a surprise packet, posted to arrive when and where least expected. Nor did we march as the British soldier does under a tropical sun, in pith helmets, half-sleeved open-necked shirts, shorts and puttees. We wore cloth caps with a peak in front and a white or khaki curtain hanging round the neck behind; thick, long, heavy overcoats buttoned right up to the throat; baggy trousers tucked into leggings; thick heavy boots and no socks. We were pretty well loaded, too, with long rifles, long bayonets in steel sheaths, very big water bottles, two hundred rounds of ammunition, stuffed *musettes* or knapsacks, containing spare kit, laden haversacks, canteens, and spare pairs of boots. But besides these things each man had some such extra load as part of a tent, firewood, or a cooking vessel; so that the top of the load on one's back rose as high as the top of one's head – or higher – and bumped against it. It took me a long time to get used to this.

No. We weren't a bit smart to look at, and there was no march discipline. We didn't march. We shuffled, shambled, staggered, tottered, strolled, rolled, bowled and pitched along anyhow. The one thing we didn't do was to straggle. The pace was set and the pace kept, and the slogan was '*Marchez ou crevez!*' ('March or die'), for if you didn't march you would most certainly die of thirst and starvation if you were lucky, or of Arabs if you weren't.

At the end of each hour the whistle blew and the little column halted for 'the cigarette space', just time to smoke a cigarette. In theory it was ten minutes in each hour.

During one longer halt, the cooks prepared a meal of a sort of stew.

In time the strain began to tell, and it was just about when people were beginning to grumble that I realized that the recruiting officer had been premature in his sarcastic praises of desert life as regards the absence of fog. For, to the appalling heat and electrical atmospheric conditions, fog was added. A beastly oppressive choking fog of dust, that diminished the circle of our horizon and rendered the almost unbearable conditions of marching even more unbearable.

'Sand storm,' said the less experienced soldiers, but the old, long-service men growled that a sand storm wasn't a sand storm while you could see and breathe and march and weren't buried alive or dead. This was nothing but a little dust!

It was truly awful anyway, and I plodded along, bent nearly double, not caring what particular name they gave it.

There was one thing to be thankful for, however. We were off the soft, shifting sand dunes, and now marching across a level plain of hard, sand-covered ground. Between us and the sky was a veil of dust through which the sun did not so much shine as loom like a great ball of brass in the hot and coppery sky. And from time to time, great blinding clouds of sand enveloped us.

I suppose it was owing to these conditions that the Arabs caught us as they did.

We had out a 'point' and flankers, of course, but presumably the flankers were ridden down when plodding along, bent double, seeing nothing but the ground, and not caring if it snowed Arabs.

They seemed to come down the wind like the dust itself. There were a few shots, a whistle, one or two orders, and thanks to Legion drill and Legion discipline, the Arab charge was met in the right way, and just in time.

My own *escouade* was unlucky in happening to be opposite

to the thickest part of the Arab line, and, in spite of the number of men and horses that our fire brought down, the remainder charged home with lance and sword, and long gun fired at short range from the hip with a weird and wild war-cry of '*Lah illa il Allah! Allahu Akbar!*' It sounded rather like a pack of jackals.

Just behind me the excellent Sergeant Krantz, a cool veteran, shouted his orders.

'Steady, now, steady! Aim low. Shoot at the horses! Aim low!' until suddenly, for the best of reasons, he stopped.

I don't really remember very much of this particular scrap. But I do remember the incredulity and the thrill at finding that I was actually taking part in a real good old-fashioned fight; just the sort of thing one had read about.

'This is what I came for,' I said to myself. 'The genuine thing! What splendid luck! A real fight with real Arabs in a real desert! It doesn't seem real.'

But it was, and we got what is known to the vulgar as a 'bellyful'. Since the first shots and shouts it was only a matter of seconds, I suppose, when, with an earth-shaking thunder of hoofs, the leaders of the charge were upon us.

Suddenly I realized that a big, bearded man in flowing, fluttering, dirty-white garments, with a nasty long lance was coming straight at me – me personally. I fired at him point blank, and apparently missed him. Also his spear missed me, due to the fact that Pierre shot either him or his horse.

Quite unwounded, I was knocked head over heels, either by this horse or another, and got to my feet as an Arab, who had reined up, or whose horse had been wounded, made a cut at me with a sword. More by luck than judgment I parried the cut, the sword striking the curved cross-hilt of my bayonet. As I drew my rifle back to lunge, the Arab whirled up his sword and cut again; and either my bayonet went in under his ribs below his raised sword arm just before the blow fell, or else Ivan shot him from behind, just in time. Anyhow, the sword cut which should have split my skull, only gave me a cut on the head.

As I staggered back, a bit dazed, a man on the ground grabbed my leg, tripped me up, and slashed at me with a dagger. He meant well – but was presumably a bit shaken by the fall that had sent his lance, rifle or gun flying from his hand – and only struck my cartridge pouch.

After an intimate minute with him I got the dagger.

Once more I rose to my feet and saw that the Arabs were in full flight – not in defeat, but according to their tip-and-run plan.

'Salvo' or rather 'Volley fire' continued while they were in sight. It was not until the 'Cease fire!' sounded that I realized what this little fight had cost me personally.

Pierre was dead. The front of his coat was sodden with blood. Hans Müller was dead, with a hideous spear wound in his throat. Ivan was dead, and, ironically in the case of so tigerishly brave a man, had his wound in his back. Torvaldsen was dead; demonstrating in death what we had known of him in life that he had a brain. Cortlandt, though not dead, was unconscious and dying, kicked on the head by a horse. Ramon was all right, and showed me the body of an Arab whom he had killed. The bayonet in Ramon's empty rifle had been bent double, and whipping out his knife, Ramon had done the Arab's business.

Kneeling beside this man, Ramon patted his face in a friendly manner.

'*A carne de lobo, diente de perra,*' he grinned, as he felt the point of his knife. 'For the flesh of a wolf, the tooth of a dog.'

There was undoubtedly a good deal of the Arab in Ramon, for the Moors owned his part of Spain for five hundred years.

I think that, for a little while at least, this violent interlude in our monotony of misery did us good.

And after a brief rest, and the somewhat sketchy burial of our dead, we marched on again, talking of our miraculous escapes and wonderful deeds, until the heat and choking dust defeated us.

At sunset the scorching wind dropped and the fog of dust slowly turned to a mere mist. When we could go no further we camped for the night, or rather for a small part of it, on a sandy plateau, scratching out a hasty square of trenches in the sand, posting sentries, and then just falling down and sleeping where we fell; many too weary even to eat.

My own personal cup was not yet quite full, as I was chosen for guard, and had to do two hours sentry-go forthwith.

Long before dawn we marched again, and when we reached the Fort it was to learn that its attackers had raised the siege and departed, probably at receiving news of the approach of the main body of the relieving force.

It was probably a tribe belonging to the besieging force who, on their way home to bed, had encountered us.

So ended, very tamely, a nevertheless sufficiently strenuous twenty-four hours in the Legion – strenuous, but not, in the eyes of survivors of the Great War, particularly hazardous.

V

THE FIRST SUBMARINE PASSAGE OF THE DARDANELLES

By COMMANDER H. G. STOKER, DSO, RN

STOKER, COMMANDER H. G. Born in Dublin 1885. Entered the Navy in 1900 and the Submarine Service 1905. Employed under the Australian Government until the World War. Commanded the first submarine to dive through the Dardanelles Straits. He was captured, made two attempts to escape across Asia Minor, but was recaptured each time and held prisoner until the end of the World War.

He retired in 1920 and since has had a successful career as an actor, playing in numerous plays in London and New York: *The Grain of Mustard Seed*, *A Social Convenience*, *Loyalties*, *Spring Cleaning*, *By Candle Light*, *Journey's End*, *Gay Adventure*. He is author of *Straws in the Wind*, A Biography, 1925; *Below the Surface*, a Naval Play (in collaboration with J. L. F. Hunt), produced at the Prince of Wales' and Apollo Theatres in 1932. He was awarded the DSO for war services.

THE FIRST SUBMARINE PASSAGE OF THE DARDANELLES

HAZARDS AND RISKS TAKEN IN the past are not really very frightening. One can face them or talk about them with complete confidence and immense bravery. There is no uneasy wondering what the deuce is going to happen.

Seventeen years have elapsed since the adventure I have to tell about, a very comfortable lapse of time from which to view the hazards and risks involved; but making it not so easy to recreate the atmosphere and conditions existing at the moment – all of which had very material bearing on the confidence and comfort one felt in facing the adventure. Because then we were facing the Unknown.

In April 1915, the allied fleets and armies were massed before the Gallipoli Peninsula. A very small unit in the vast Armada was Submarine AE2, of which I was in command.

Most men present realized the magnitude of the task on hand. If it was possible to force the Dardanelles it would now be done, and the sooner the business started the better.

The Dardanelles Straits connects the Mediterranean with the Sea of Marmora, on the further shores of which lies

Constantinople. It is thirty-five miles long, and half a mile wide at the Narrows of Chanak. A continuous current runs through it into the Mediterranean.

At that time it was heavily mined, and its banks were studded with forts. No surface ship could pass through it except by kind permission of the Turks until mines and forts were destroyed, and it was the general opinion of officers present that it was equally impossible for a submarine to get through.

Submarine B 11, commanded by Lieutenant Holbrook, had made an attempt to penetrate as far as the Narrows – some ten miles or so in from the entrance. She got under the first mine field, and found an enemy to torpedo when she had gone seven miles; but she then got into such difficulties with diving control and other technicalities that she had to turn back.

However, she was of the B class boats – considerably smaller than the E class; and we in AE2 believed that it might be possible to dive right through the Straits and into the Sea of Marmora at any rate there was sufficient chance of success to justify the attempt being made.

The difficulties were obvious enough, the total distance an E boat could dive was fifty miles through the water. Would this distance be sufficient to carry her through a strait thirty-five miles long when a current of three to five miles an hour was running against her? Arithmetic said no, but one hoped that the current was strongest at the surface and would become weaker at a depth – though there was then no information on the point.

Then there would be mines. A submarine can dive underneath mines, but only by going to such a depth that her periscope is submerged and she is therefore blind. Constant

Australian submarine AE2 arriving at Portsmouth to prepare for her voyage.

observation, however, would be needed in navigating through the narrow Straits, and to accomplish this she must come near enough to the surface for a mine to strike her. It was possible, too, that there were other obstructions of various sorts in the Narrows and also off the dangerous Nagara Point a few miles higher up.

Another thing was that the submarine would, almost certainly, be sighted when passing through the Narrows, and must expect the enemy's small craft to make every endeavour to harry and, if possible, ram her during the remainder of the passage.

Finally, there was the difficulty of navigating, while submerged, through a strait whose narrow passages, angle turns, and strong currents made it none too easy a matter even in a surface ship.

We persuaded ourselves that the passage might be possible, that the unknown and problematic dangers could only be proved by someone going to try them, and that the value of success was such that it would be justifiable to risk a submarine in the attempt. However, it was one thing to persuade ourselves and another to persuade other people. A formal application to make the attempt was not favourably received the Admiral apparently shared the general view that the feat was impossible. We were very disappointed because by now our hearts were set on it.

A few weeks passed, three new E class submarines came out from England, and, while AE2 was refitting at Malta, E15, under Lieut.-Commander Brodie, was permitted by the Admiral to attempt the passage. She penetrated five miles, then she was swept by the current on to the southern shore, was hit immediately by the Turkish guns, her captain and a number of the crew were killed, and the remainder made prisoners of war.

On April 21 we rejoined the Fleet. Two days elapsed, days electric with anticipation for fleets and armies, for April 25 was the date fixed for the main attack to commence. And then we received a signal saying that the Admiral wished to see me on board the flagship at once.

Aboard the *Queen Elizabeth* I was received by the Chief of Staff, Commodore Keyes. If I still believed it might be possible to dive through the Dardanelles I would be allowed to try. He took me to the Admiral, who was kindness itself. Without belittling the difficulties he simply asked how we proposed to overcome them. He found it difficult himself to believe the feat possible, but its military value would be so great that it must be tried. If we got through the other boats would immediately be sent to follow. Finally, he wished us luck, and concluded: 'If you succeed there is no calculating the result, and it may well be that you will have done more to finish the War than any other act accomplished.'

I hurried back to AE2, where we immediately commenced to take in extra provisions and prepare for sea. Two hours later we were threading our way out through the crowded harbour and passed the flagship – from whose quarter-deck the Admiral and Chief of Staff waved their farewells and God-speeds in person.

It was after midnight when we made our way to the Dardanelles' entrance – a lovely night, clear and calm, with a fair-sized moon and myriad stars casting their ghostly light on the smooth water.

Our plan was to enter the Straits after the moon had set, and proceed slowly along on the surface – slowly so that our wash, showing white in the darkness, would not attract attention from the shore; and on the surface, so as to conserve electric power for diving. We hoped in this manner to cover some miles without being discovered by the enemy. Then, at break of day, we would dive.

As we arrived abreast the entrance the moon had still a small distance to go before dipping into her silvery bath.

We waited by the side of the black and sinister-looking destroyers, while the perfect stillness of the night seemed to heighten the tension of the moment. And then the moon touched the horizon, and was gone. In the darkness we crept away from the destroyers. One man only was on the bridge with me, all others below ready for instant diving, as we followed our course in the centre of the Straits at a speed of seven knots.

Two enemy searchlights on the southern shore were sweeping the waters with their long rays; further on the more powerful searchlight at the Narrows threw beams of a yellower hue as it searched the higher reaches. As we drew nearer and yet nearer to the first light it seemed as if progress on the surface must soon be stopped if we were to remain undiscovered.

And then the Goddess of Fortune smiled; the first light spluttered and went out. We crept along with a renewed sense of security. And then, almost too unbelievable to be true, the second light quietly faded out. It seemed tremendous luck – we could now in practical safety follow our surface route much further than we had ever dreamt possible, perhaps right up to the main minefield.

On and on we crept until, of a sudden, the maddeningly clear rays again shot across the water. It would mean instant discovery to remain on the surface, so we must dive. I closed the conning-tower lid, gave the order to flood the tanks, and went below. And then – moment ripe – an accident happened. The shaft which worked the foremost diving rudders broke: impossible to mend under several hours work, impossible to dive, impossible to go on. We must turn back! After all the working up to that moment; with a job before us that might have important bearing on the finish of the War; a chance of a lifetime before us – well, one did not like having to turn back. We raced along at full speed, trying to regain the open sea before day broke and the enemy opened fire.

The cold light of morning showed up plainly and more plainly on the shore as we passed the entrance and rejoined the watching destroyers. We proceeded to an anchorage and feverishly set to work to make good the damaged shaft. By afternoon it was repaired, and all was ready again. But would we be given a second chance?

Towards evening the *Queen Elizabeth* arrived, and the Admiral sent for me. If I'd had a tail it would most certainly have tripped me up as I climbed on to the flagship's quarter-deck. But kindness again was all I met. 'It was very bad luck,' the Admiral said. 'You did well to get so far. Try again tomorrow. If you succeed in getting through, there is nothing you could possibly want that we will not do for you.'

There was, however, to be a minor alteration in the orders. The morrow was the day of disembarkation of our attacking army. Battleships would be in the entrance to the Straits covering the landing, and therefore the enemy would probably launch floating mines against them. So, instead of trying to pass through unseen, AE2 was to attack and sink, if possible, any mine-dropping ships found.

'In fact,' said the Chief of Staff, 'generally run amuck at the Narrows – if you get there.'

If you searched the world over I doubt if you would find a more unpleasant spot to carry out a submarine attack than this Narrows at Chanak. Half a mile wide, with the current running at its strongest, it is certainly not an ideal place for manoeuvres in a comparatively slow-moving and slow-turning submarine. Also the thought that we ourselves might meet one of these floating mines hardly added to the entertainment the day was likely to provide for us. However, we were either going to get through or else we were not, and an extra difficulty or so at this stage did not seem to make very much matter. But as it turned out the new order had a far-reaching effect on our after life.

Three a.m. on Sunday, April 25. It was absolutely dark, still, and dead calm as AE2 entered the Dardanelles Straits again and crept along on the surface. With broken clouds shutting out such light as a moonless sky gives, the searchlights seemed more powerful than before. One felt forced to edge away from the lights and nearer to the northern shore. Each time a beam of light touched AE2 with brighter and yet brighter finger, we held our breath. Would the steady sweep pause for a moment, and show a suspicion of our shadowy presence? There was no hope of reaching as high a point as on the previous night. But as we got used to the eerie feeling caused by the passing light, a necessitous boldness forced us farther and farther along, now at dead slow speed on one engine.

Suddenly there was a BANG, and the broken swish of a shell as it hurtled past close to my head. We had edged too near the northern shore, and been sighted by the lookouts of a gun battery. Within a minute we were submerged. Above us the darkness prevented sight through the periscope, but a faint glimmer of light in the eastern sky gave promise of approaching day. At dead slow speed, and at twenty feet, we dived along on our course, until the gathering light showed giant contours of the hills on the northern shore. Then we lowered the periscope and plunged to seventy feet for the passage through the main minefield. It is difficult to describe our experiences and feelings during the next hour. The rappings and scrapings on the hull of the boat by the mooring wires of the mines, held taut by the buoyancy of the mines themselves overhead, seemed most damnably continuous. One ought to be fairly safe when well submerged, but there was always the chance of one of the wires catching on a projection on the boat's side and dragging its mine, with a bang, down on the top of us.

On two occasions something hard – much harder than

the wire – hit the bows, and then went tap, tap, tapping along the boat's side. We imagined, uncomfortably, that they were mines failing to explode. Once some object got caught up forward and remained knocking insistently on the starboard bow. For several minutes we all listened to it in uneasy silence before it broke away, tapped along the side, and followed the rest of our enemies astern.

Twice we rose in the minefield for hasty observation and quick correction of course, then back to the safer depths. The observations showed we were progressing at faster speed than anticipated – the current was evidently much weaker at the seventy feet depth. Even so, I was agreeably surprised on rising the third time to find we were already through the minefield. The Narrows were only three or four hundred yards ahead.

The revised order to attack mine-droppers now obliged us to keep the periscope up for a considerable time to take stock of the situation.

The surface of the water was a flat and oily calm, so the periscope was immediately sighted, and a heavy fire opened from the forts on either side. The shock of projectiles striking the water overhead caused subdued thuds in the submarine, while shrapnel bullets falling through the water on the boat's deck sounded like hailstones. The water around the top of the periscope was lashed into white spray. The effect was curiously pretty, but added little to the ease of taking observations.

An old battleship hulk from which mines might be dropped was anchored abreast Chanak. Higher up the Narrows, approaching at high speed, were a number of destroyers and small craft.

I decided to attack the old battleship, so I lowered the periscope and edged towards her. As soon as we hoisted the periscope again the hail of fire re-opened, and a small cruiser came hurrying out from behind the hulk. Now this was just the kind of vessel that would be fitted as a mine-dropper, and from the course she was following it seemed she was trying to drop mines across our bows. Obviously a better quarry; so I got the sights on at a range of 30 yards and fired the bow torpedo at her. One of the destroyers was now very close, attempting to ram us on the port side, so at the moment of firing I ordered seventy feet. A last glance as the periscope dipped showed the destroyer apparently right on top of us, and then, amidst the noise of her propeller whizzing overhead, came the big explosion as our torpedo found its mark. We had now two dangers to think about; the danger of not being deep enough to avoid the destroyer and the danger of becoming entangled in the sinking ship ahead – as a ship of that size must be expected to sink very rapidly. So we altered course a point to starboard with the object of passing astern of her.

The risk of remaining off one's true course for any length of time in such narrow and fast running waters was obvious, and after three minutes we altered back to what seemed the correct course for regaining the centre of the Straits. At the same time I ordered a rise to twenty feet for another observation.

We had risen to perhaps forty feet when the submarine struck bottom hard, and slid quickly up to a depth of ten feet. Through the periscope I observed that the position was on the eastern or Asiatic shore very close in, right under the guns of a fort. As I looked, one of the guns fired, its flash coming right round the periscope. It gave the impression that it was firing straight into my eye, so that I involuntarily jumped backwards from the periscope eyepiece. I lowered it quickly and we tried to refloat the boat.

Now, when the depth gauges indicated ten feet there was a considerable amount of the conning tower and bridge of AE2 above water; indeed, the tops of the periscope pedestals, being the highest objects, were almost ten feet clear of the surface.

With the boat apparently fast aground and a continued din of falling shell, the situation looked as unpleasant as it well could be very like the end of the story. An eternity of time seemed to pass. In reality it was only five minutes before the boat began to move; but even in that time it seemed inconceivable that we were not hit. I afterwards learnt that the guns of the fort could not be depressed enough to bear on us, but the other forts and ships must have made very bad shooting to miss this standing target.

The efforts which eventually proved successful to slide the submarine down the bank left her heading down the Straits again, and we had to turn a half-circle to get her back on her proper course. At a depth of seventy feet we went ahead on the port propeller, helm hard aport, and dived off the bank trying to turn as quickly as possible. A few minutes passed, while propellers rushing overhead caused pleasant thoughts of the trouble we were making; then we swung rapidly to our proper course and went ahead on the starboard propeller.

Bump! From a depth of seventy feet we slid gracefully to a miserable eight feet. Where on earth were we now? Through the periscope I observed that AE2, with an apparent liking for forts, had chosen one on the western shore under which to run. The cursed current, which had swept us across to this point, relented for a moment and helped us by swinging the boat's stern round to port, leaving her grounding more aft than forward, and with an inclination down by the bows. A quick glance round showed a gunboat and some destroyers, little more than 100 yards off, blazing hard with all their broadsides, a cluster of small boats which we guessed were picking up the survivors of the sunk cruiser, and then, best of all, a clear view up the Straits showing that if we could only get off we were heading on the right course.

Full speed ahead both motors! Ominous noises from aft made one fear the propellers would get smashed, but on we must go; and, after a shake, then a move, then another shake, AE2 gave two great bumps and slithered down to thirty feet, having been four minutes at the eight-feet depth. Again the escape must be considered little short of miraculous.

Away, then, at seventy feet, with a host of small vessels in close pursuit. The two severe bumps might have caused leaks in our ballast tanks, and we feared the submarine might not be under sufficient control diving; but all seemed well, and, after a spell, we rose to twenty feet to observe.

Right ahead was Nagara Point – the last of our navigational obstacles involving a nasty right-hand turn. Surrounding us were the pursuing vessels – a gunboat, some destroyers, and a number of tugs and small craft. We could only spare time to fix our position accurately before the destroyers, in attempts to ram, became dangerous. Then away to seventy feet.

Now came the problem of rounding Nagara Point. If we grounded while near the surface for observation we could not hope to escape again; and we would also be in more

THE FIRST SUBMARINE PASSAGE OF THE DARDANELLES

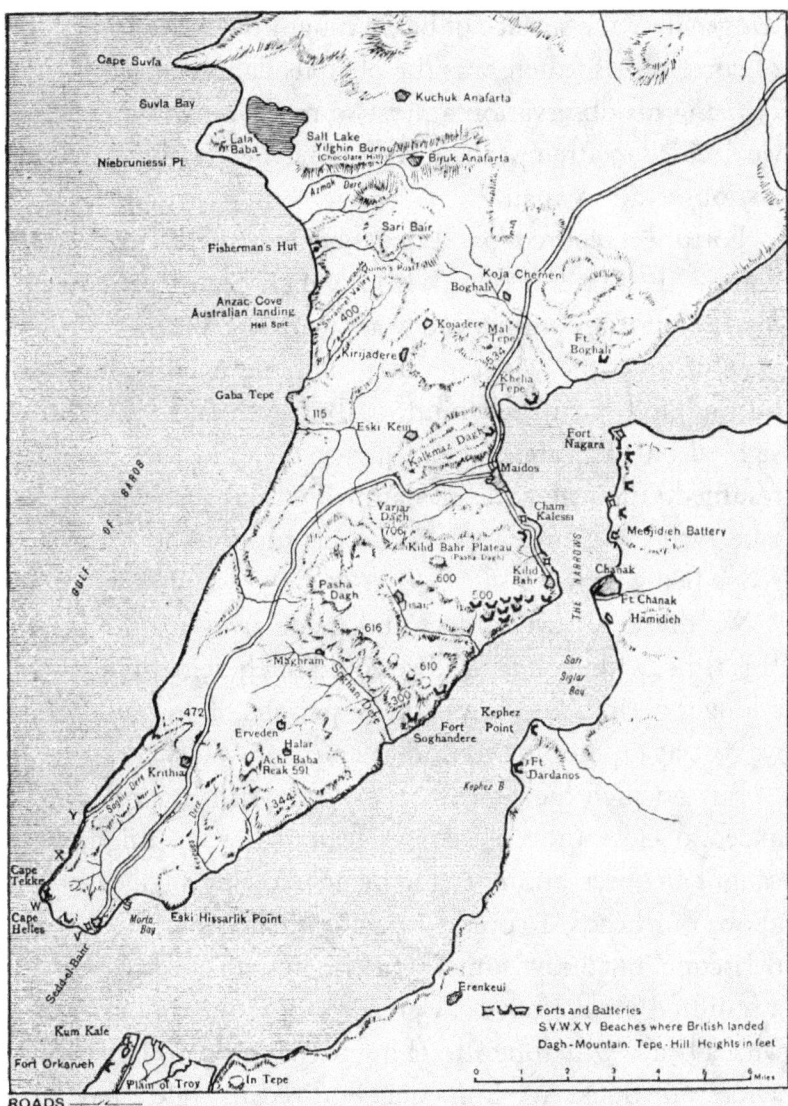

Map of The Dardanelles at the time of the Great War.

danger near the surface of being caught by swirls and eddies of current. Also there was the obvious danger and difficulty of rising for observation amidst so many pursuing craft. So we decided to attempt the turn at ninety feet without making any observation at all.

Fortune favoured us, and when we rose again Nagara Point – the place, it is said, from which Leander's semi-submarine efforts commenced was abaft the beam, we were heading into the wider reaches, and the enemy ships still hurried and scurried behind us. But even as I looked they sighted our periscope, their guns spoke, and the chase was resumed. The water was so damnably calm that we couldn't take even the shortest spell of observation without the periscope being seen.

We dived to seventy feet and made away up the Straits. This time, with a clear run, we could safely remain below for a longer period, and it was three-quarters of an hour before we rose again, hoping to find the pursuit well shaken off.

But no such luck – the enemy were still in close attendance, so close indeed that we feared that we might have caught an observation net and be now towing a tell-tale buoy above our heads. I couldn't see any such buoy through the periscope, but I saw something else instead. Just ahead, not a hundred yards from us, were two tugs, one on either bow with a heavy wire rope stretching between them. It was right across our track. We immediately dived to eighty feet, and turned off to starboard to consider the situation.

The more we thought, however, the less pleasant it seemed. These tugs were laying a trap of some sort, and no doubt there would be more such traps during the twenty-odd miles which we still had to go before we were clear of the Straits.

The longer we remained in their unpleasant company the more chance there was of some ordinary diving accident forcing us to the surface and to instant destruction. If we'd caught an observation net our end was certain in any case, and so it was delaying the inevitable to go on. So we turned at right-angles and ran direct for the Asiatic shore. We knew there was a bank which shoaled slowly there, and so we approached it at dead slow speed and grounded and rested on the bottom at a depth of seventy feet.

The most anxious period of the day followed. Had we caught an observation net? If so, we were marked, and the end must come soon. And even if we hadn't, the enemy had only to carry out intelligent sweeping operations of the few places a submarine could hide on the bottom, and they would have only too good a chance of finding us.

It was about 8.30 a.m. when we grounded. An hour later a ship passed overhead and there was a knock at the boat's side as a sweep hit and jumped over us. We were excessively lucky it didn't catch up!

Soon afterwards other ships passed, and this O went on at regular intervals. One of these vessels was obviously a single-engine ship and its solitary screw made an easily recognizable noise. We named him Percival. Percival's repeated passages over us were trying for the nerves, and the fact that we were well out of the track of ships following their ordinary course up and down the Straits proved that Percival and his friends were searching for us.

We decided we must move to another place in the hope that the passage of ships overhead would cease. But the diving control of the boat had been lost. The bumps from the last grounding had evidently so strained her that several of the ballast tanks were leaking. It was most difficult to regain control without coming to the surface.

We made several unsuccessful attempts, and then had to resign ourselves to staying where we were, helpless, until darkness could permit us to rise to the surface and – enemy also permitting – readjust the ballast tanks.

Time moved beastly slowly. Percival and his friends passed and repassed at steady intervals. Attempted jokes as to his reappearance fell mighty flat. The few moments immediately after his passing were the bad ones. If any sweep he was dragging after him caught up, the side of our boat would be blown in on us.

All things come to an end. At 6.45 p.m. – that's to say after about ten hours of this anxiety – Percival passed to pass no more. Two hours later AE2 rose to the surface after being submerged over sixteen hours.

We found a bright moonlight night overhead; but, to our relief, no enemy ships in sight. Our position was about half a mile from the Asiatic shore, in the sweep of the bay which lies above Nagara Point. Marshy swamp land, devoid of habitation afforded safety from observation from the shore. It was unlikely that ships from the centre of the Straits could see us against the land. The only danger of discovery now lay in being found by a vessel patrolling the coast during the three or four hours necessary for us to remain on the surface for recharging batteries.

Now, too, we could signal the Fleet. A dramatic moment, that, as we watched the damp aerial wire throwing purply blue sparks as the longs and shorts of the call sign were flashed. But the answering call never came. Wireless in submarines was very unreliable in those days. It was of the utmost importance that we should get into communication with the Admiral and tell him that the most difficult part of our task was accomplished. Whether any other submarines should be risked would depend on the success or failure of our attempt, so he must know as quickly as possible that we had now practically succeeded.

This wireless failure was a very great disappointment. All that we could do was to flash out our signal in the hope that some ship would pick it up. And this we did. (Years afterwards I learnt from Admiral Keyes that our signal was received at a critical moment during a Council of War on board the *Queen Elizabeth*, and the news that a submarine had got through altered the whole tide of the discussion.)

We resumed our passage up the Straits before dawn, proceeding slowly on the surface. When the gathering light showed clear enough for an observer to sight us from the shore we dived once again.

Objects were just beginning to take definite form through the periscope when I sighted two ships approaching, obviously men-of-war, one in front of the other; the leader, as far as I could see in the bad light, was the smaller; both had two funnels. They were not far off, and the periscope, which was making a big white wash, must be lowered, for the water was still absolutely calm, unmarked by a ripple.

Steering a parallel and opposite course to the enemy, we approached, and when judgment estimated us to be within torpedo range, hoisted the periscope. Right abeam was a ship, looking mighty big at a range of 500 yards, and I jumped to the conclusion that she was the second, or rearmost ship. The bearing for firing the port torpedo was on, and we fired. The ship dodged, the torpedo passed ahead of her; and then, looking round, I found to my disgust that I had fired at the smaller of the two ships. The other was following, but it was now too late to bring any of the other tubes to bear with good chance of the torpedo hitting. We had lost a glorious chance, and through my fault alone. Of little use to think that two sleepless nights and the experiences of the previous day hardly tended to produce the even, balanced mind necessary to successful submarine attacks in these unsuitable conditions of bad light and smooth sea. We had had a glorious chance, and it was gone. Terribly disappointed we dived along on our course, forming a resolve to find a quiet spot for rest before carrying out another attack.

Towards seven o'clock we approached Gallipoli town, at the head of the Straits. Stretching in endless chain from shore to shore across our course was a quantity of small boats. Plunging to seventy feet we passed peaceably beneath them, and so dived out into the Sea of Marmora.

Our wish was realized. The submarine passage of the Dardanelles was not only proved possible but made.

AE2 had other hazardous adventures, but space doesn't permit to tell of them. In the end the enemy guns got her. She now rests at the bottom of the Sea of Marmora; and within her lies a case of most excellent port – which we had never opened.

VI

ROUNDING UP THE TURKISH BRIGANDS

By CAPTAIN H. C. ARMSTRONG, OBE

ARMSTRONG, CAPTAIN H. C. Commissioned to the Indian Army 1912: proceeded to Mesopotamia on active service. Captured at the siege of Kut-alAmarah and held prisoner until August 1918. Subsequently was Assistant and Acting Military Attaché to the High Commissioner, Constantinople, and Supervisor of the Turkish gendarmerie in the Scutari area.

Resigned from the Army and was appointed Assessor to the Commission for the Assessment of Damages Suffered in Turkey. As such travelled extensively throughout Cyprus, Syria, Palestine, Arabia and Turkey. Author of *Turkey in Travail, Turkey and Syria Reborn* (Bodley Head) and *Grey Wolf: Mustafa Kemal: An Intimate Study of a Dictator* (Arthur Barker, 1932). Awarded the OBE (Military) for war services, while a prisoner, and the Bronze Medal of the Royal Humane Society for saving life at sea.

ROUNDING UP THE TURKISH BRIGANDS

'HULLO! HULLO! KIM, OH!' I sat up suddenly on my bed as the Turkish officer across the room answered the Field telephone. 'Who's speaking?' 'Sergeant Ali! Yes, Ali! What is it?' The Turkish officer was Captain Hussein, the Commander of the gendarmes of the Scutari district, and I was there to help and advise him. It was two o'clock in the morning of August 1, just ten years ago. The night was stifling hot, and we were sleeping in our clothes in the office, waiting for news.

Hussein turned to me. 'It's Ali Chaoush, Sergeant Ali, you remember him! We put him in charge of that new outpost we made on the edge of the forest of Alemdagh. He reports that brigands raided Yahoudi Keuy, the Jewish village, about three hours ago. There's no exact news, but he thinks it was Karaoglan's band.'

'We'll go at once,' I said.

'Ali,' he called down the telephone, 'send your men patrolling along the edge of the forest, and meet me in the Jewish village this evening.'

Hussein and I had a tough job ahead. Our district was a part of Asiatic Turkey about the area of Cornwall. On the west the Bosphorus separated us from Europe and

Constantinople. To the east the district ran on into the interior of Turkey, which is an immense wild country of mountains. On the north and south was sea. There were well-to-do towns and villages along the shores. These were easy to handle; but the country inland was all mountains and forests and very difficult. The people were mainly Turks and Greeks, with a few Albanians, Jews and Lazzes, which are mountaineers from the Black Sea coast. Each of these nationalities kept to itself and lived in separate villages, and they were all at daggers drawn.

The Greeks and Turks were always killing and massacring each other. The district had been in the throes of civil war for years, and it was overrun with brigands. The Greek villagers helped the Greek brigands, and the Turkish villagers helped the Turkish brigands. No man's life was safe, and no one dare go outside a village alone. The Turkish Government had lost control, and the brigands had made a reign of terror.

Our job was to wipe out the brigands, and disarm the whole area, for every villager had a rifle or revolver hidden away somewhere. This was the only way to restore confidence, law and order, so that the civil government could take over control again and bring back peace and prosperity.

We had spent four months preparing ourselves in the town of Scutari, and had enlisted and trained two hundred men. Now we were ready.

The biggest band of brigands was to receive our attention first: the little ones could be dealt with easily afterwards, and the biggest band of Greeks in the south was under this brute Karaoglan, about whom we had just received news.

We had been waiting for this news. Karaoglan's band had broken up in the spring and gone into the coast towns and

Constantinople to enjoy themselves as long as their money lasted. But we had learnt from a woman spy that he had summoned his men again, and was planning some new raid, but we could not find out *where* they were to meet and *what* he was after.

Now we knew. He had raided the Jewish village, about twenty miles away cross country, and we must get on to his track at once and smash him.

The horses were soon ready. We could hear them stamping and fidgeting in the cobbled courtyard, and dawn was just showing grey in the sky as we came down the rickety stairs of the gendarmes' headquarters. Across the Bosphorus we could hear the sounds of the great city of Constantinople waking, the rattle of chains as they closed the bridge over the Golden Horn and the hooting of the steamers. A gendarme held my stirrup as I adjusted my revolver on my hip and swung up into the saddle.

We turned inland, and clattered out over the cobbled streets, leaving Constantinople behind us. Captain Hussein and I were leading, and Hadji Ramazan, the sergeant, rode behind me. Hadji was a tough old man, very religious and The Turkish absolutely loyal and honest. The Turkish Government very rarely paid the gendarmes, and as Hadji would never take a bribe, his clothes were threadbare and his toes stuck out through the ends of his riding boots.

A Turkish gendarme is half a soldier and half a policeman. He is drilled and armed like a soldier, but he is responsible for patrolling the open country and keeping law and order as a policeman does inside the town. Most of the gendarmes are on foot, but a small proportion are mounted, and they supply their own horses. No gendarme ever travels alone.

Usually they move in pairs, or sometimes in patrols under a non-commissioned officer.

But to come back to the story.

Alongside Hadji rode Sidki, the corporal. He was a clever and amusing rascal, and we all knew him as Sidki the Liar. He thought a tremendous lot of himself, and rode with a swagger, his black fez stuck on one side of his head; now and then he would look at himself in a pocket looking glass and give his moustache a twirl. If there was a good-looking woman about, he would make his white stallion buck to show off, but he had plenty of initiative and ability.

Then came fifteen gendarmes with their rifles slung across their backs. They were all mounted on stallions which bucked and kicked and squealed and fought to get close to my mare, but she was English and no slut, and promptly kicked any stallion that got near her.

So we went down those old streets of Scutari making an uproar like a mixture of a circus and a battery of guns going into action.

We crossed a vast cemetery full of cypress trees outside the town, and then, as the sun rose, we went up over some low hills on to the plains, beyond. They were dried up and ankle-deep in dust, and as the sun climbed up the sky, the heat became intense. But we rode steadily all that day and soon saw the effects of brigand rule.

Many of the villages we passed were deserted; the houses were falling down and the fields uncultivated. Where there had been telegraphs the wire had been cut down and the poles chopped up for firewood. The roads were a succession of potholes and all the bridges were broken. The few people we met salaamed to us with a hangdog look of fear.

We reached the Jewish village towards sunset and Ali was waiting for us there, but with little news. The headman of the village and all the villagers denied any knowledge of brigands or raids.

But Hussein knew his work. He went down the village street listening from door to door. Suddenly he went into one of the houses. Then he called me to follow. A black cloud of flies rose, filling the room. There was a man lying in the corner with his head and shoulders beaten to a pulp, and on a bed with a child beside her was a girl, moaning to herself. She was stripped to the waist, and her arms and breasts were ribbons of raw flesh. She had been beaten with the sharp edge of a knife.

'It's Karaoglan all right,' said Hussein. 'That's a little trick of his to make them talk.' We came out and called the headman and the elders of the village again, but still they wouldn't speak. They were terrified. They had not even dared to call a doctor for the girl on the bed, and they had probably meant to bury the man secretly as soon as it was dark.

Then Hussein threatened to beat them all, and that made them talk, but only under the pledge of secrecy.

The raid had been made, they said, by Karaoglan and twelve men. He had also had with him the well-known brigands, Zaffiri, Christo, Nikola and Yanni. A month ago some refugees from the Revolution in Russia had come to the village. They had been rich in Russia, and were believed to have brought jewellery and gold away with them and hidden it in the village. The dead man and the girl on the bed were two of the refugees. The brigands had been after the treasure, but they had found nothing and had gone off westwards towards the village of Bakal, swearing that they would come back and burn the Jewish village if the jewellery wasn't produced.

We halted for the night and set off for Bakal before dawn. Our luck was in that morning. As we moved down a valley we saw a man with a rifle slung over his shoulder half a mile ahead of us. He looked back, and at once darted off towards some scrub forest where the horses could not follow him.

However, we made straight after him at a gallop, helter-skelter across a bit of plain, down into a dry river-bed full of rocks and up the hill beyond, kicking up a cloud of dust. My mare put one of her clumsy great feet into a hole, and she and I came down with a crash. I sat up half-stunned and saw the gendarmes catch up with the man and beat him down with their whips as he turned and tried to unsling his rifle.

He was Yanni, one of Karaoglan's companions in the recent raid. The gendarmes took him away up a valley, and there they beat him until he talked. I neither looked nor listened, but I would not interfere, for I remembered the girl on the bed in the Jewish village.

He told us that Karaoglan and his men were up in the forest, watching us to see what we were going to do, and how strong we were. They were expecting us to visit Bakal, and as soon as we had left it they would probably go there themselves for rest and food.

This information suggested a simple plan to us. We went into the village of Bakal, carried out a perfunctory search and then marched off north as if we were going to a place named Alemdar. As soon as it was dark, however, we turned back on Bakal to surround it.

We got back to Bakal just before dawn, and as soon as our men were in position I left the horses in the valley, climbed a hill and sat down to wait for the light.

Suddenly I saw something moving in a field of maize below me, just outside our ring. I focussed my glasses on it and saw it was a man creeping along with a rifle in his hand, and after him came another and then another. The brigands were stealing a march on us. I blew the alarm, and they

Captain H.C. Armstrong, OBE, with Captain Hussein Hasni, Commander of the Scutari Gendarmerie.

jumped up at once and burst into full view, running hard. Unfortunately we had loosened our horses' girths, and by the time they were ready and the gendarmes up the brigands were five hundred yards away among the mountain gullies.

Then came the gendarmes riding hard and firing from the saddle, with Sidki in front on his white stallion. The air was full of ricocheting bullets, and focussing my glasses on the chase in front, I saw the three brigands separate. Two ran up towards the mountain, and one came doubling back. Sidki was close behind him, but the brigand turned, fired and hit the white stallion, which fell with a crash. Poor Sidki was out of action, but after the brigands came two more gendarmes and Hadji at full gallop. They had orders to capture and not to kill, so when they came abreast of their quarry they hit at him with the loaded butts of their whips. But the brigand ran with incredible speed, dodged into a ravine full of boulders and disappeared.

Then I saw him again, and he was coming my way. I caught up a rifle and rushed to intercept him. He was running in skin shoes so I was no match for him in my heavy field boots. But for a second I saw him clear, took a snap shot, and missed him.

It was Karaoglan himself, a huge gorilla of a man, dark and handsome to look at, with long arms and a tremendous chest. We had lost him, but the gendarmes had caught the other two men, who turned out to be Christo and Nikola. Sidki was unhurt except for a bruising, but we had to shoot his white stallion.

We then went into Bakal again. There was no pretence this time about our search, and we found rifles, revolvers and ammunition everywhere. The headman and priest were pathetic. 'We want peace and security like anyone else,' they said, 'but what else can we do? There's been no government here for a long time. It is true you are here now, but tomorrow perhaps you'll go away, and the brigands are always with us.'

We had struck the first big blow, and we now set to work to win the confidence of the villagers. When they saw we meant business they began to talk, and bit by bit we got the name and description of each brigand.

The band itself was somewhere in the Great Forest, and since it would have taken about one thousand men to search it, our only alternative was to try to starve them out by cutting off their supplies. This wasn't easy, for they still had relatives and friends in the villages who gave them help.

We devised another trap. In the open plain some five miles from the edge of the forest there were several villages in a group, the biggest of which was called the Pashas. Between these villages and the forest was a range of steep hills with only one path through them. We withdrew all our gendarmes from these villages and concentrated them in every other direction, especially in the villages in the forest itself or those close on its edge. In this way, bit by bit, we reduced the brigands' possible sources of supply in every village except the Pashas' group.

One night we caught four men in the forest carrying sacks of bread and groceries to a rendezvous with the brigands. We waited at the rendezvous, but the brigands had been warned and didn't turn up. But that night they must have gone without food, and next night they raided through the hills into the village of the Pashas.

We got the news even before they were there, raced the mounted gendarmes across country in the dark, picketed the path through the hills, and sent out sentries and patrols. Then we waited.

There was no moon, and though the sky was alive with stars, we were in pitch darkness close to the ground. The air was heavy and windless. We waited hour by hour straining into the darkness. Nothing happened.

Then suddenly we heard the clang of a rifle dropped, away to our left, and a sentry came running in to say that there was a file of men moving over the hills in that direction. The brigands had discovered another route. We doubled back with all speed, and as we came round a corner of rock they opened fire on us. The bullets crashed and echoed against the rock, and a gendarme close to me went down with a thud and lay groaning. The flashes showed that there must be at least twenty brigands in front of us.

We began to work our way carefully round between them and the forest, but all of a sudden we were fired on from behind. It was one of our own patrols who had got lost in the dark and thought we were the brigands, and in the confusion the real brigands escaped.

We had one man killed and four wounded, but we had taken eight prisoners. However, we were sold all round, for our prisoners turned out to be innocent villagers whom the brigands had forced to act as porters.

The only satisfaction we had was to find that the ground was strewn with bread and groceries which had been thrown away in the general scrimmage.

We found the village of the Pashas completely gutted. The brigands had come in hungry and savage. They had beaten everyone they met, cleaned out the shops and the houses, and thrown what they did not want into the streets. Food had been their main object, but they had also taken any valuables they could lay hands on, tearing the gold rings out of the women's ears and off their fingers, and even chopping off a finger if there was any difficulty. Some of them had found liquor and gone wild, raped some women and played old harry until Karaoglan had got them back in hand. And finally they had carried off a rich Turk as hostage, boasting that they would kill all the gendarmes first and then take revenge on the villages afterwards.

But they had made one mistake. One of their principal supporters lived in this village, and some of the drunken brigands had insulted his wife, and, when he protested, beaten him and chucked him into a ditch. This man wanted his revenge, and he knew Karaoglan's 'hide out' in the forest. So we took him with us and set off at once with twenty foot gendarmes under Hussein and Sidki.

We travelled that day and the next night on foot by very narrow paths. It was nervous going, for the undergrowth was thick and we went blind, and during the night a great storm came bursting down from the Black Sea, making the paths slippery and soaking us to the skin. It was followed by a wind that drowned out all other sounds.

On the second day we came to a hill in the forest. Its base was covered with scrub, but the upper slopes were bare, and there was a hut on top. This, our guide said, was Karaoglan's retreat.

It was very well placed, for a sentry up above couldn't fail to observe anyone coming up, but we couldn't see any signs of life. We would have to rush it. The gendarmes fanned out and crawled through the scrub. Where it ended we rested to get our breath, and then at a word from Hussein we raced up, and Sidki kicked in the door.

In the gloom inside a dozen men leapt up, but we had them covered. They made no resistance. They were Karaoglan, his lieutenant, Zaffiri, and twelve men of his band.

Our luck had been in this time. Karaoglan was quite unprepared; he was asleep, and his sentry outside had been bending down to roll and light a cigarette. The howling wind had covered all our sounds.

We handcuffed the brigands and roped them together, and brought them down the hill. In the scrub we found the skeletons of two men the band had murdered and we took these with us also. Three days later we reached the gendarmerie headquarters at Scutari.

The same night Karaoglan was beaten and then locked in his cell with the two skeletons. That broke his nerve and he confessed in detail to eighty-six murders.

We handed the whole band over to the Central Prison in Constantinople to await trial, and many weeks later I heard that Karaoglan was dead. It seems that all the prisoners had been locked together in one large cell, and one night they had quarrelled, torn down the electric light and fought in the dark. Karaoglan had wrenched a nail out of a wall to defend himself with, and had left his mark on every other man in the cell before they pulled him down and kicked him to pieces.

The rest were hanged in the public square in due course.

After that we routed out the other nests of brigands. Bit by bit the roads were rebuilt, the telegraph lines remade, and the people coaxed back to their villages; and where there had been desolation and terror, security returned and the villagers tilled their fields and harvested their crops in safety.

VII

FACING DEATH ON THE GEORGES SHOALS

By WESTON MARTYR

MARTYR, WESTON. Story writer. Began gathering material for his stories by running away to sea at the age of fifteen. to see the Boer War. Ran away from his ship Became a gold miner and prospector in South Africa, a labour recruiter in China and a business man in Japan. Bought a schooner and traded in the South Seas. Fought in France with the 1st Sherwood Foresters and a Tunnelling Company, R.E. Continued his search for writing material in various parts of the world, notably amongst head hunters in Formosa and bootleggers in New York. Has now settled down to write about what he has learnt.

Favourite recreation is making ocean voyages in small sailing boats.

Books: *The South-Seaman, Not Without Dust and Heat, The £200 Millionaire* and various short stories.

FACING DEATH ON THE GEORGES SHOALS

I HAPPEN TO HAVE SPENT a good part of my life sailing little boats about the big seas. It is a game that appeals to me, and I can say in general it is not the hazardous business most landsmen appear to think it. The last voyage I made, for instance, was in a cutter (a small one-masted sailing yacht), from Falmouth to New York and back to Plymouth, via the Bermudas; a double crossing of the Atlantic. The outward passage lasted fifty days, and it took only twenty-eight days to sail home again. That whole business was a matter of less than ten thousand miles, a few gales of wind, and all the meat aboard going bad in the middle of the Atlantic. Nothing much to make a song about, and a mere picnic compared with the shorter voyage I propose to tell of now.

This voyage was from a small harbour on the east coast of Nova Scotia to Vineyard Haven in Martha's Vineyard, Massachusetts, in all only some three hundred-odd miles – not a long passage, you see, and I hoped, with luck, to make it within four days. The time was the first week in March, which is really rather too early in the year to go sailing about those seas in a little boat; because in March in Nova Scotia it is still winter, when gales of wind are far too apt to occur, and where sometimes a blizzard – a freezing, killing hurricane – sweeps down out of the Arctic to devastate that part of the world.

However, I was in a hurry – which is usually a mistake. The boat in which I sailed was a thirty-foot schooner – that is, she had two masts and four fore-and-aft sails – and if you will pace out ten paces on your carpet, you will see how long or short, she was. Three good paces will show you her greatest breadth, and if you are over five feet six inches tall you would certainly bump your head on the deck beams every time you tried to stand upright in the cabin.

Which thought gives me an idea. I think it will make this story more realistic if you, in imagination, make this voyage with me. Step aboard, Shipmate! Come below, and shut the cabin hatch after you, for it is perishing cold on deck. If you will sail with me to Vineyard Haven we should have a good time. You can take the starboard bunk. The mattress smells slightly of iodine because it is stuffed with dried seaweed. It sends you to sleep. When you lie down on that you have got to sleep. And here are half a dozen Hudson Bay three-point blankets. If they do not keep you warm nothing will. Forward here is the galley, with a big coal stove; for I like to keep things below as warm, dry and comfortable as I can. Aft of the cabin there is this forty-gallon tank of fresh water, and enough food and stores for the two of us for three weeks.

Will you come? Do not be apprehensive at the smallness of the boat. She is small, but she is good. She is strong and well built; and I have sailed about the high seas in many worse boats than this during the last thirty years and never come to much harm yet, touch wood. The truth is, any small boat, be she well-built and properly handled, is as safe during bad weather at sea as any big luxury liner. This is a fact, which has been proved repeatedly.

I could give you a number of instances, but one will do. In 1901 John Voss sailed all the way around this world in the 38-foot dug-out canoe *Tilikum*. He sailed over 49,000 miles rode out in perfect safety twenty-two major gales and enjoyed himself thoroughly – all that, mark you, in a dug-out canoe. In comparison our boat is a fine big ship, and our voyage is only 300 miles. So there is not a thing to be scared of.

If you are a lady, so much the better, because I remember one of the very best shipmates I ever sailed with was a girl. She pulled her weight all the time even if it was only eight stone. But she made every ounce count. She stood her watch on deck, turn and turn about with me, every four hours, fine or blow. She did her half of the work of the ship; and there was no nonsense about her not turning out on deck in bad weather, nor of her doing all the housemaid work or the cooking just because she was a woman. No! We shared the job. And, anyway, I was a darned sight better cook than she was. And I know of three cases where women have lasted out long small-boat voyages better than their men. Will you come? Good! We sail at daybreak tomorrow, so I advise you to follow my example and turn in now for an all-night sleep. We may not get another chance.

We sleep and you awake at dawn to sniff with appreciation two of the most divine incenses known to man – I allude to the smells of hot coffee and fried bacon. We enjoy our early breakfast and then we go on deck, and while you are heaving up the anchor I set the sails.

Within five minutes we are gliding out of the little harbour before a light land breeze that smells deliciously as the pine forests ashore. In an hour we begin to warm up in the sun. are six miles out at sea, well clear of the coast – a line of low cliffs, topped with pine woods and fringed with reefs and detached rocks, against which the great swells, rolling in from the North Atlantic, break in thunder and a wild white turmoil of foam.

It is a bad coast to be caught on, so we set a course to pass ten miles clear of Cape Sable, the most south-easterly point of Nova Scotia and now distant from us twenty-five miles.

I regret to see that you are looking rather apprehensively at those swells. They are rolling in majestically from seaward and they must have been caused by a heavy gale of wind out there. But they are not breaking here. Their tops are round and smooth, and all they do to our small boat is to lift her up for twenty feet or so and let her down again into the troughs. Well, what of it? It is as safe as a switchback, and much more pleasant. So long as the crests do not break there is nothing to worry about. The swells themselves, I assure you, cannot hurt us.

Consider, for your comfort, that it is not the actual water in the waves that comes charging at us, it is only the form, the *shape* of the waves that move. And how can a mere shape hurt us?

So be bold! If you wait until we lift on the top of a swell you will just be able to see a white lighthouse on a little island. That is Cape Sable. And it is eight bells-noon. Here! Take the wheel. Steer west by south. It is easy and you will soon get the hang of it. Keep that point on the compass card opposite the black line on the compass case. That is our course for Nantucket. We have got 250 miles to go before we get there – say two days more, before we sight land again. So, till then, we have got nothing to worry about. We cannot hit anything if we try – except the Georges Shoals. But they lie a good fifteen miles to the south of our course, thank Heaven.

We do not want to hit *them*. They are sand shoals, but you cannot see them because they are submerged. They lie out in deep water, one hundred miles from Nantucket. There is less than ten feet of water over them in places, and in fine, calm weather we could probably sail right across them without coming to much harm, perhaps, if only we dared to take the risk. But in bad weather the Georges is a terrible place. The seas break everywhere on the shallower patches and any vessel caught there in a gale of wind could not last ten seconds. So I am glad we pass fifteen miles off the beastly place.

Now we will have our lunch and then I will have a nap till 4 p.m. All you have to do in the meantime is to steer a straight course and call me if the wind changes or if you do not like the look of the weather.

Wake me at four o'clock, when I'll take charge till eight. Then you'll be on watch again till midnight. We'll stand watch and watch. Four hours on and four off. It breaks one's sleep, but you'll soon get used to it.

Thus we carry on, through the afternoon and the night. You find that your watch on deck from eight to midnight passes quickly. You have acquired confidence in yourself and in the boat by this time. You can steer a straight course now with one hand on the wheel and one eye on the compass. In fact, you begin to fancy yourself as a sailor. And as for the boat, she has not as much as taken a drop of spray on deck, in spite of the big swell; and the cheeky, buoyant way she rises as the great hills of water overtake her shows you she thinks nothing of them at all. The wind is fair, a good whole sail breeze and between the clouds the stars are showing. All round you it is pitchblack darkness, and you feel very much alone and a little awed as you think of your situation – far out at sea, in the night, in a boat so small that you have but to stretch out your hand to touch the face of the mighty deep. But the tiny light shining on the compass is a comfort to you – and you laugh to yourself when you look in through the cabin hatch and see me down there, fast asleep and snoring hard. At midnight you wake me, and I relieve you at the wheel. You go below and lay yourself down and in an instant you are fast asleep.

You awake, amazed, to a world of sound and fury. You start up in your bunk and the violent motion of the boat nearly pitches you out headlong. You hear wind whistling in the rigging, the angry roar of breaking waters and the great crash of a sea hitting the planking within six inches of your head. You hear a faint shout and, struggling to the cabin hatch, you slide it open.

Immediately the noise is multiplied tremendously and, for a moment, you are daunted. Then you look outside and a shower of spray strikes you in the face. It hurts. It is as though someone had thrown a handful of gravel at you. You see me braced at the wheel, with cascades of water running from my oilskins. Behind me rears a grey-green hill of water, hoary with foam and spindrift, bearing a roaring angry crest. Then the hill of water vanishes as the stern of the boat flings up to a sky all sinister greens and evil copper, blotched with purple-black cloud. Down goes the stern, revealing another great wave baring its teeth at us and when you realize from my urgent gestures that I want you to come on deck and steer, you are dismayed. But only for the moment. By the time you reach the wheel you are wet to the skin and the wind seems striving to tear your hair and clothes off you. I cry in your ear:

'Steer her dead before the wind'; and such is the power of the wind that to you my shout seems to come from a great distance.

You steer. It is hard work to steer. The wheel kicks viciously, and tries to tear the spokes from your hands. But you steer. It takes most of your strength and all of your mind to keep the boat running before the wind. As each sea roars up behind her she struggles to turn round and face the thing. But you check her each time. You know if one of those waves catches her broadside on that it will sweep right over her and wash us and everything on deck away. You keep the boat running before the seas. You steer with all your might and all your faculties. And presently you become aware of a struggle, a fight going on beside you.

It is me, battling with a berserk sail. I am trying to stow the main, the biggest sail in the boat. I drag it slowly down the mast, a flapping, slashing maniac of a sail. A child can stow it in an ordinary wind, but *now*! It is a savage thing, and dangerous. But at last it is down and lashed and double-lashed to the boom.

For minutes I sit on the deck, clasping the mast, panting, catching my breath, licking my wounds. Then I crawl, slowly and fearfully forward, flat on my belly like a snake, and tackle the two head sails. The instant I start to lower the jib the canvas gives two savage flaps that shake the whole boat, and then the sail disintegrates in whipping threads and tatters. The fore staysail comes down easily enough; but it takes an hour of wary, weary effort to double reef the foresail.

An hour and nearly all my strength; but I have enough left when the job done, to crawl to the wheel, bring the boat's head round to the wind and heave her to.

We watch her anxiously for some minutes. Under her one small triangle of sail she now faces the seas, lifts herself over them as they come rushing at her, gives way before them when they threaten to come crashing down upon her deck. She does well. She is all right. Hove-to like this she can look after herself for a while, so we lash the wheel, then crawl down into the cabin, played out, done to a turn, with no more strength left in us.

According to the clock it is 10 a.m. – three hours since you came on deck! It seems like ten minutes. And the fire is out. And the cabin floor is a foot deep in ashes, stores, blankets and *water*! Heaven help us, we've sprung a leak! For a little we gaze at each other in consternation.

To spring a leak at sea is bad enough at any time; but in our present circumstances it is a calamity. However, calamity or not, we have to tackle it, and, played out as we are, we must pump. So we pump – a backbreaking job – and after a while the pump refuses to work. The suction is choked by the ashes washed out of the stove. As we can't pump we must bail with buckets, which is harder work even than pumping and gives less results. But we bail for our lives. And presently, when we begin to feel we might as well drown quietly as go on any more with that heartbreaking, hopeless labour, we notice there is not quite so much water in the boat as before.

We are gaining on the leak. In time we bail the boat nearly dry and suspect that there is no leak after all. And when it becomes clear that most of the water must have come in through the cabin hatch, which someone forgot to shut, a great weight is lifted from our minds, and we become almost cheerful – but not for long.

It is hard to be cheerful when everything, including yourself, is sopping wet in a temperature only just above freezing. Our bailing has made us sweat – one does not perspire in such circumstances, one sweats good and plenty. So very soon we are shuddering in the bitter cold and our teeth chatter. I try to light the stove. It is a long job, because somehow or other in my struggle with the sails I have managed to sprain one thumb and tear the nail off the other; also the kindlings are wet, and most of the matches. However, some paraffin poured into the stove does the trick in the end, and in the strong draught the flames go roaring up the stove pipe.

The heat is heavenly and we huddle close to the stove. But not for long. We can feel that things are not going well with the boat. The whistling of the wind has changed to howlings. The vibration of the rigging makes the whole boat shake and every time she rises to the top of a sea the wind knocks her flat, in spite of the tiny area of sail she is carrying. And now she cannot rise soon enough to all the seas. They begin to break aboard, and down in the cabin the sound of them as they crash on the deck is frightening. The boat is being overpowered.

Every minute the weather is getting worse, and soon she will be overwhelmed, unless we help her. We must relieve her by stowing the reefed foresail and putting out a sea-anchor. This is a daunting thought. Down in the cabin we have to hold on hard and brace ourselves even to remain seated on the floor, so who can be expected to go out on the open deck and fight with sails and ropes in the face of all that fury of the wind and sea? It isn't fair! It seems futile to make the effort, absurd. Better to drown quietly in the cabin than be swept off the deck to die struggling in all that uproar and brutal violence out there.

Then we look at each other – and feel guilty and ashamed of our unspoken thought. We crawl aft and drag out from a locker, with groans and curses, the sea anchor and its coil of thick rope. We gingerly open the cabin hatch, and gasp and slam it shut again against the torrent of icy water that instantly bursts in against the roar and fury of the gale against all those things that terrify us out there. We hesitate. We tremble in each nerve and muscle and fetch deep shivering sighs. And then, thank heavens, our desperation, or something, suddenly makes us angry. Cursing, we fling open the hatch and scramble out. On deck the wind takes our breath away. We bow our heads and gasp hang on like grim death.

And then I scramble madly forward along the deck with the end of the anchor rope. Out there I feel like a soldier who climbs from the comparative shelter of a trench, out into the bareness, the noise and the violence of a no man's land filled with bullets and bursting shells. I am desperately afraid and desperately anxious to get the job over and done. I dare not look at the seas. Every ten seconds I hear the roar of one coming and clamp my legs and arms around anything solid I can reach.

A giant plunges me beneath Niagara, holds me down, shakes me viciously, tries to wrench me from my hold and in between whiles I find myself frantically bending on the anchor rope to the bow bitts.

At last it is done and I make violent motions at you and you understand the time has come for you to put the sea-anchor over the side. I see you wrestling with the thing in the wind. It is a bag of the stoutest canvas, eight feet long with its mouth held open by a steel ring. Into the water it goes and I watch you almost follow it, without so much as one quicker beat of my heart. You were nearly lurched overboard, but narrow escapes have long ago become part of our natural order of things. *I* can't help you. The vital thing is, what effect will the sea-anchor have?

It sinks and I see the boat carried down wind of it between the scend of two enormous seas. Then the anchor rope tautens with a wrench and jerk and swings the boat's bow to wind and sea. It is doing its job, by heavens and by that same token I had better finish mine. With the boat held head on to the sea it is now less difficult to work on deck. I lower away the foresail in frantic haste and the canvas comes down, slatting and thundering in the rush of that mighty wind. I subdue the mad sail with ropes, and throwing caution to the winds, dive for the cabin.

You have dived, too, and together we poke our heads out of the hatch, watching with anxiety how the boat will now behave. And she does well. With her bow held up to the seas by her sea-anchor she takes less water on deck, and under her bare poles she is no longer knocked down by the wind every time she climbs a sea.

But heavens above! how she rolls and pitches. She flings herself thirty feet up the face of each sea, pitchpoles over the crest and falls another thirty feet into the valley beyond.

And she rolls, rolls, rolls – through one hundred degrees and more, every two seconds. It sickens us to watch her. It seems as if she soon must shake herself to pieces, shake her masts right out.

We notice for the first time that it is and has been snowing heavily. The snow and spray are beginning to freeze to the rigging. We shut the hatch and jam ourselves between the berths on the cabin floor. Even there we are flung about unless we hold on hard. But the stove is still alight – which is lucky, for we understand now it is not an ordinary gale we have been caught in; it is that terror of those seas, a blizzard. And without the stove it would freeze us to death tonight.

We are wet through, bruised all over and exhausted. We lie down on the floor. The wind howls like a pack of wolves, screams like a maniac, booms like great guns. Sea after sea hits us with a rending crash and the motion is unbelievable, terrific. And we lie there, hour after hour, trying to stop ourselves from being rolled about, craving, yearning for quietness, some rest, some peace, knowing those things to be all equally impossible.

But in the night we both nearly attain peace – almost, but not quite. And if we had, our rest would have been for ever. For the wind affects the draught of the stove and the fumes, instead of going up the pipe, are blown back into the cabin, where we have shut tight every opening to keep out the water and the freezing cold.

After we seem to have been lying there for years in misery, I begin to notice a nasty taste of sulphur in my mouth, but I ignore it for a delicious feeling of numbness has come over me and I think, I hope, I pray that at last I am actually going to sleep. To sleep! If only you would stop breathing so noisily, so stertorously. You sound, confound you, like someone choking in a fit.

And then, suddenly, I understand. I reach the hatch somehow and open it and fall half outside in a faint. And when I come to I am stupid and nearly frozen, but I have enough sense left and enough strength to drag you half out of the hatch, too. When we come to our senses we put out the fire – and lose the warmth, our last comfort. We wrap ourselves up in the wet blankets and some spare sails, and suffer for fifteen ghastly hours, wherein the bitter cold is harder to bear than the fear of death which also never leaves us.

Suddenly, in the middle of the next day, something comes through to me from the pandemonium outside – a change in the noise, in the motion the sensation of something impending is so strong that this all but frozen corpse springs up alert, intense, listening. Through the noise of the wind comes the sound of the furious waters; but the seas are roaring no longer they are crashing all round us, and the boat, instead of being flung from hollow to crest is being stamped on, savaged, kicked aside. I open the hatch and look outside and my heart stops beating. For the water is green no longer. It is brown! And our decks are covered with sand! This is the end. We have been driven into shallow water. We're done for. We're on the Georges Shoals!

Man is a queer creature. Before the prospect of pain and suffering he is very apt to squeal and give up. But face him with almost certain and apparently inescapable death, and as likely as not he will put up a good fight for his life. I have noticed this peculiar psychological reaction frequently, especially during the War. And it is so with us now. We are in water so shallow that the sand on the bottom is being churned up by the waves. And down wind, dead to leeward of us, and no more than a quarter of a mile off is a shallower patch still. We can see that by the breakers. The waves are having a sort of savage dogfight there. The spot is chaos, awful to look at, and we are drifting right down on it fast. It is better to do something than just sit and wait to be killed.

Without any consultation, one of us saws through the sea-anchor rope with a knife, while the other hoists the foresail half up. We don't believe that any boat can possibly sail in such a wind and sea and we certainly cannot sail into the wind and away from those terrific breakers. But we may, by some miracle, skirt them if we try. And presently we find we are doing, actually, that very thing! The miracle is happening! The breakers are slowly passing to one side. They are desperately close – but they are passing. They *have* passed. Well done, good boat.

But we do not congratulate ourselves. We have now sailed right amongst the shoals. At the moment we are in a less shallow part, but on each side of us, and ahead, and astern, too, now are more and more shoal patches, with the breakers roaring over them in a way that is frightful to see. We must simply try to keep in the deeper channels and thread our way through the maze ahead if we can. It seems absurd to try it. But it's all we can do. It's thousands to one against us; but we've dodged one bank already – and we may again.

So we carry on; a forlorn hope indeed, driven on by the gale behind, watching the breakers ahead, turning now half right, now half left, side stepping disaster by yards, dodging destruction by feet, missing death by inches, waiting as we fall into the hollow of each and every wave for the shock of our keel striking the bottom and our boat being instantaneously shattered to splinters.

Time does not exist under such conditions of hazard and

mental strain; but we know it took us four hours to cross the shoals. And the dark was falling when the face of the waters changed from brown to green and told us we had escaped from that Valley of the Shadow.

VIII

LOST IN THE JUNGLE

By G. W. T. GARROOD

GARROOD, G. W. T. Enlisted at the beginning of the World War: promoted to a commission. He was engaged in the fiercest fighting at Gallipoli. At Achi-baba he was laid out for burial, but providentially a doctor found he was alive. Subsequently he was transferred to the Flying Corps and employed in France, the Cameroons, German East Africa and Egypt. Since the war, he has had a very successful business career.

LOST IN THE JUNGLE

I WAS JUST NINETEEN WHEN I arrived in East Africa in 1916. I had already been wounded at Gallipoli, learnt to fly and seen service as a pilot in the R.F.C. in France. A Medical Board. had then said I was to go to a warm climate, and personally I was 'all for it', so I was posted to No. 26 Squadron of the Royal Flying Corps in East Africa.

I arrived at Mombasa with two other pilots, with many quaint ideas and many keen desires between us about big-game hunting. East Africa was one big-game preserve that was how we pictured it, and it was just a lucky coincidence that numbers of our then enemy had colonized German East Africa, now Tanganyika territory, and we had to do something about turning them out.

However, a very industrious Squadron Commander at once interfered with our big-game ambitions, and we were soon very definitely mixed up in the war business once again.

Our landing ground was a small clearing in the bush at a place called Tulo, just south of the Uluguru Mountains, and I set out from there one afternoon to bomb a place called Logi Logi.

Logi Logi is on the south bank of the Rufiji River, about forty-five miles due south of our landing ground. One of our infantry columns had reached the north bank, but further up the river.

By flying west from Tulo for thirty miles and then south, we could keep in touch with our column's lines of communication, and if we were obliged to make a forced landing we had the chance of running into some of our own fellows. However, with the optimism of youth I shunned this precaution and flew due south over the intervening stretch of country which was totally uninhabited and as thick in parts as the African jungle can be.

I was about three miles from Logi Logi when my engine began to cough and splutter. I eased the throttle, and then tried jerking it to clear it; but I knew it was ignition trouble, and in a few seconds my propeller stopped and my precious 800 feet of altitude was down to 600. I selected a 'nice green oval stretch of grass' to set the plane down upon; but at 200 feet I remembered my bombs. It would be risky making such a speculative landing with a one hundred pounder, four twenty-five's and two petrol bombs, so I released the lot. A few seconds later, before the echo of the bomb explosions had died away, I had pancaked the bus (that means a slow landing so that she does not run far) on to my 'nice green oval stretch of grass'.

It really had looked ideal from the air, but to my consternation the grass was six feet high, and the machine turned up on to her nose. It was a bog and the water nearly covered the top of the landing wheels.

My first impression was of the eerie silence which sent a shiver through my spine. Then some kind of bird screeched, as a sort of protest I supposed, at my noisy intrusion into its preserves. Well! I didn't want to intrude anyway. I knew of many nicer places, I thought. I suppose I must have remained perched up there in the cockpit for a full minute before I made any movement, and then that chilling silence began to get on my nerves.

Before I climbed out I opened the little cupboard behind my seat and took out my revolver, ammunition, sun helmet, water bottle and bottle of quinine; also a tin of sardines and a packet of chocolate that I had stowed away a few weeks back in case of this kind of emergency.

It had already dawned on me that I was in for a long tramp, as I knew full well that there was no place where a machine could get down to pick me up, and I was positive there wasn't a village for forty miles. I then removed the compass and took a long lingering look at the instrument board. But I left this and the eight-day watch.

I then decided it would be wiser to make tracks due north for the Uluguru Mountains and the Military Road that ran

Crashed BE2c of the type flown by G.W.T. Garrood in East Africa.

along its slopes, rather than trek due west to strike our column's lines of communication. The distance would be much the same either way, but by striking north I would be less likely to barge into any enemy patrol, which might be sent out from across the river if they had seen me come down.

It was now about 4.45 p.m. and I resolved to make for the nearest lot of trees, which were about two hundred yards away, and try and do two hours' hiking before dark. I let myself down into the water which I was pleased to notice did not come above my knees. Unfortunately I had had a bout of malaria three days previously and was not in cross-country form. I reached the trees and found there was much less water there. I might explain that at this season the heavy rains were on.

It was here that I first noticed elephant spoor, and I learnt afterwards from the pilot who first spotted my machine from the air that there was, in fact a large herd close by. It did not take me long to realize how valuable my compass was, since the growth was very thick, and I frequently had to turn back and try another course.

I had not done more than about half a mile when night came on and my trek ceased rather suddenly. Not twenty yards ahead an ugly black animal about four feet high faced me with vicious-looking tusks. Although I had managed to recognize elephant spoor I really knew nothing about wild animals and had not the foggiest idea whether this one was dangerous or not. However, I figured that the most intelligent thing to do was to scramble up the nearest tree, which I did. The animal crashed off into the undergrowth, and when the noise had died away there again fell one of those silences that made me shiver.

I had chosen my tree rather hastily, and did not much care for it, but before I had time to look around for a better one it was quite dark. So I tried to make myself at home where I was. I changed my position in the tree, wedged myself into a fork, and hung my equipment on nearby branches. But hard though I tried to make myself more comfortable, the bough I was seated on did not co-operate.

At about 7 p.m. it thundered for a few minutes and then down came the rain. It took about half a minute to drench me to the skin and then it went on for nearly an hour. As soon as the rain left off out came the mosquitoes. I was wearing shorts so my knees were bare to every hungry mosquito, and they were all hungry. The insect world then commenced to chant and a few frogs croaked. I thought longingly of my very comfortable grass hut at Tulo with its bed and white sheets. Never mind, I would be sleeping in it tomorrow night for certain, I told myself.

At about nine o'clock my thoughts were interrupted by the distant roar of a lion. I grasped my revolver and cocked the trigger and sat there hoping that the black animal with the tusks I had seen gave off a more attractive scent for lions than I did. The roaring ceased, the insects stopped their chorus and once again the awful eerie silence descended.

At about ten o'clock I tried hard to doze, but I had hardly closed my eyes before the sudden snapping of a twig nearby opened them again. The moon had just broken through the clouds, and there down below, about thirty feet away from my tree, were what looked like two green electric bulbs. I gripped my revolver, and a curious fit of shuddering took me. The two lights moved in a circle around my tree. They made no noise, and I thought I might be lightheaded or dreaming, so I shut my eyes several times and then opened them, to convince myself that the lights were real. I thought of firing my revolver, but as the rain had drenched everything I was afraid that it might not go off. If I did not attempt to fire it, I could persuade myself that it *would* go off if I wanted it to really badly.

Meanwhile the eyes continued to circle, disappearing for a few seconds and then appearing again. This went on for nearly ten minutes, but it seemed like ten hours. The shuddering gripped me again and my nerves were absolutely at snapping point. So many miles of jungle separated me from the nearest human being; but as I reverted to this thought something seemed to give way inside me and I suddenly found myself yelling at the top of my voice. It was quite involuntary; I just somehow lost control. Instantly there was a noisy crackling of the undergrowth, the eyes disappeared, the leopard had scuttled.

A feeling of shame at my fearful exhibition then crept over me, and I tried to get back to the same note of the yell I had let out and made it coincide with the beginning of the last line of 'Oh, you beautiful doll'. This singing business seemed good stunt – I sang every song I could think of and some confidence slowly returned. Then I got on to hymns, and when I was not sure of the words I improvised – and how I dragged out those 'Amens'.

Strangely enough I began to see the humorous side. Here was I in the pitch darkness perched fourteen feet above the ground in an uncomfortable tree, surrounded by wild animals, wet through, frogs croaking all round, terrifying noises, then uncanny silences – here I was singing 'All things bright and beautiful; all creatures great and small'!

At about 3 a.m. I began to get hungry, but as I had had two good meals inside me before coming down, I resisted the temptation to gnaw at the chocolate, though I had a drink from my water bottle. The hours crept on and another eerie silence preceded the dawn. A gentle breeze made a rustling sound up in the trees and soon it was grey; the insect world grew silent, and day had come.

As soon as it was light enough to see I descended my tree and collected the articles I had dropped during the night. It was about 6 a.m. when I pushed off, keeping to my compass course. My khaki drill tunic and my shirt, shorts and puttees were wet through and I felt clammy. I crossed two streams, which I had to swim, and at 8.30 I was confronted by a substantial river running east and west.

I came to the conclusion it would have to be crossed, so I chose a sharp bend to strike out from and trusted to the current to swing me to the other side. The jungle was so dense on both sides that I could not throw my clothes across. I put the revolver and food in my tunic pockets, rolled the tunic and buttoned it round my neck, so that the revolver would have a chance to keep dry, and tied my boots to the back of my belt.

In this guise I pushed off. I had not swum more than a few yards from the bank, and was only just keeping pace with the current, when I turned my head during one of my strokes, and saw not ten yards from me the unmistakable nose of a crocodile.

In the excitement and the extra energy used at the sight of the croc's nose, the tunic round my neck came undone and sank with the weight of the revolver and other equipment, but I reached the bank.

As soon as I was out I watched the croc churning the water in all directions, but as I stood there looking on, there was a movement in the bush and a huge hippo appeared, snorting vigorously. I had never seen a hippo except at the zoo, and this one had no bars in front of it. I hared up a tree and the noise I made caused the hippo to come and investigate. He remained at the foot of the tree for a full minute, while I marvelled at his huge bulk and appalling ugliness; then he snorted contemptuously and waddled off.

I was now without food, firearms, or compass, and I started off again through the most awful undergrowth imaginable. My progress was heartbreaking. At the end of the first hour I was not one hundred yards away from the river. The bush scratched my face, arms and legs unmercifully, then it commenced to rain again and I had a two hours' tropical downpour.

I struck further west after this, and at last found a game path where the going was better. My stomach was rumbling, but I had not a thing to satisfy it with. Then my head began to throb and I imagined I was in for a return of fever. The game path finished abruptly in a bog which I soon found was knee-deep. Since I had no compass now I climbed a tree and saw that if I crossed the bog I could be trekking due north towards the Uluguru Mountains, which made an excellent landmark. I found the bog an awful sweat, and when I reached a piece of slightly raised ground I fell down as I was not feeling too good. In another hour I was on dry ground again.

While I was resting here the drone of an aeroplane engine electrified me into activity, and I tore off my shirt ready to wave. The plane loomed up a mile away, but did not see my antics, and disappeared leaving me lonelier than ever.

Shortly after midday I started again and found rather more open country, except for short thorny bush which had no pity on my knees. I swam two streams between one and two o'clock, losing my puttees in the second. My legs were now bare to all the thorn bush and sword grass through which I passed, to say nothing of myriads of flies. There was a most tiresome fly with a long thin body which drew blood. The only good thing about them was that they did not seem to mind being swotted, and I subsequently learnt they were blind and infest all bog country. Another discomfort was a pain in my neck, which I developed through continually turning my head quickly to see if I was being followed.

I was drinking now from streams and any odd pool, but the food question was speedily becoming serious. I waded up several streams, and searched in vain for eggs in some coconut-shaped birds' nests which were built on the rushes. At about four o'clock I crossed another stream, but the bush on the other side was too thick, so I recrossed, a little further west. This was the seventh swim in one day, not counting the ditches up to my armpits.

Then I sat down again for a rest. The sun was still well up, so I took off my shirt and shorts and spread them out to dry. I was lying down with just my helmet, vest and boots on when a breaking of bush sounded behind me and the snort of another hippo. I was getting careless, inasmuch as I was near no tree, but I sprang up and ran for a clump about 300 yards away. I had plenty of time to climb up one, but it was dark before I was sure of the hippo's departure. This tree had no convenient fork into which I could wedge myself, so I descended, and just had time to break off a few big leaves for a bed and some for a cover, when total darkness set in.

It was only about six o'clock, and of course I could not sleep, so I just sat up against my tree and thought rather a lot of depressing thoughts. I got through three songs and a chorus of a hymn which I had a vague idea I had heard the Salvation Army singing something about 'Count your Blessings' – and this cheered me up for a bit. Then my head began to throb, and I remembered the quinine which I had tucked into my helmet some weeks before. My forehead felt so hot that I thought a dose would do me good, but within three minutes of swallowing it I was violently sick.

During the night I developed that 'fed up fever' feeling. At one time a lion roared less than 500 yards away it seemed, and I heard the trumpeting of elephants. I suppose I must have lost consciousness for half an hour or so. I was losing interest in life anyway, and nothing short of a definite attack from something would have made me climb that tree again.

The second night finished somehow and daylight came, but I must have dozed on for another hour. I then went to find my shorts and shirt, and although I am positive I returned to the same spot where I had laid them out, they were not to be found. Perhaps some baboons had made off with them; at any rate, there was nothing to be done now but to carry on in what scanty attire remained to me.

I felt rather anxious as to how I would feel when I started to trek, but I was able to get going. I passed through a fairly open piece of ground about midday and came across two huge buffaloes. I stood quite still and they moved off. A little further on I disturbed a family of giraffes, but they ambled off, peering back at me occasionally around the top of some trees, and I daresay I must have presented as ludicrous an appearance to them as they did to me.

In the early afternoon I struck the most awful bush I came across the whole time. It consisted chiefly of very thick thorn bush, up to nine feet high, and interspersed with sword rushes. The thorn bush fastened on to me in the most painful manner imaginable, and the sword grass slashed and cut me. I forced my way through it for about half a mile, as I had seen from a tree-top an open space beyond it and the Uluguru Mountains in the distance. I reached the open space and crossed it, but only to find myself facing another large river at least seventy yards across. I just sank down on the ground, knowing quite well that I was too weak to swim it.

While I rested here I decided that I must have something to eat and chewed away at some stems of grass. Then I retraced my steps and again marched due west through the same type of thorny scrub, hoping that the river either ran north and south or would narrow. I nearly stepped on a huge snake about twelve feet long, but it was sleeping or dead; I did not try to discover which.

I planned to take a more north-westerly course in the hope of avoiding the river; then a machine circled around two miles away, but went off in a southerly direction. By four o'clock, after passing through country rather like parkland, I was faced with what looked like an open plain about a mile across. I set out to cross this before dusk, but found to my disappointment that it was only another bog similar to the 'nice green oval patch' I had put my machine down on.

A solitary tree about halfway across was now my objective before dusk. I had no desire to spend the night in the water, and as night came down I reached the tree, which I was pleased to discover was on comparatively dry ground.

As I approached it I heard the chattering and jibbering

of baboons, and about a dozen of them streaked down the tree and disappeared into the grass. I just had time to break off some leaves to make some kind of a bed when it became pitch dark.

For the first two hours of darkness a terrible depression fell on me; words kept occurring to me from the burial service: something about 'dust to dust' and 'worms and bodies decaying'; then I wondered whether, if I died, I should ever be found, and so on. At this stage I really began to believe I should not get through. The last time I had seen the mountains they seemed as far away as ever. Then I thought another song 'wouldn't do me any harm', and the next thing I remembered was the sun shining down. So passed the third night.

I felt better in myself after the sleep, but when I stood up I realized how weak I was getting. By about eight o'clock I was on my way and struck some thick bush again at midday.

It was here that I noticed every now and then the flapping of wings behind me and realized to my consternation that two vultures were following me. This frightened me badly at first, and then braced me up quite a bit. I selected a young bough of a tree as a cudgel and determined not to give in whatever happened. The vultures never came very near, but flapped from tree to tree, and even when I could not see them I felt that their ugly faces were peering at me just the same.

I met with another bog beyond the thick bush, and by this time it must have been two o'clock. I thought I could get through it in an hour, but I found I needed a rest every few minutes or so. The vultures still followed me. Often the water was up to my hips, but usually around my knees. It was while I was struggling along in this way that I came across a kind of bamboo fence sticking up out of the water.

My excitement knew no bounds, as I realized that nobody but a human being could have made it. Perhaps I was getting near a native village, so I let loose a series of long-drawn-out 'Hullo's'. Attached to the fence were some contraptions like lobster pots and I found several fish like mackerel in one of them. I took one out, killed it, ripped it open and tried to eat it just as it was, for I had no matches to make a fire. But raw fish was not a success and I was soon violently sick.

As soon as I felt strong enough I sent up some more feeble 'Hullo's', and threw another of the fish to the vultures. Then I struggled on again, but this struggling was getting slower and slower, and every minute or so I had to sit down where I could with my mouth above water.

I don't know how long I went on like this – I'd lost sense of time – but suddenly I thought I heard an answering 'Hullo'. This revived me as nothing else could; then doubts began to grow and I thought it was a parrot mocking me. It came again and again, that cry – was it a cry? – sometimes quite near, sometimes it seemed miles away. I went on 'Hulloing' as lustily as I could. I could only see above the tall grass in some places, and I felt as though I was going to give way again, as I had up in the tree the first night.

Then without any warning the grass quivered over on my right and two small black natives appeared, armed with hunting spears, and advanced with their 'Jambo' or 'salutation'. I expect my appearance shocked them a bit. I was just wearing a vest, sun helmet and boots; my legs and body were almost covered with mud, mixed with the blood that had oozed from a number of cuts; and I had four days' growth of beard and sprouting from my neck were some leaves which I had tucked in my vest to protect a wound from the sun. I had stuck one of the gutted fish on top of my sun helmet in the hope that the sun would cook it, and in my hands I carried my young tree-cudgel.

I explained in broken Swahili that I was a Big Bird Chief, and that my Big Bird had been taken ill and I had marched for three days and was very hungry. They at once offered to take me to their village where there was much food, and with one on each side of me we set off in a south-westerly direction for over an hour, away from the mountains, resting every five minutes or so.

I realized that if I had gone on in a north-westerly direction I should have left their village on my left. I also learnt that they only came down at a certain time once every four days to take the fish from the nets, so this had been another piece of luck for me.

At last a dry patch was reached with evidence of cultivation and I was soon in the native village. It consisted of one large grass hut and about a dozen small ones. I staggered into the large hut and flopped down on some rush mats. Mealie meal was brought along in a 'calabash'. It was steaming hot and I consumed three helpings. Mealie meal is Indian corn pounded into flour and then mixed with water. It tastes as one imagines billposter's paste would taste, but I was told afterwards that it was the finest thing I could have had. I asked if my fish could be fried, and this was detached from my helmet and cooked in some very unsavoury fat; but I thoroughly enjoyed it.

The Headman's wife then appeared with some hot water and sponged me down, which was very painful, but afterwards some thin and very soothing oil was rubbed into my cuts. Night had now come on and in spite of some acute tummy pains I was soon asleep and the next thing I remember was the barking of dogs round about midnight. It turned out that soon after my arrival at the village, the Headman had sent a runner into Dethumi – eight miles away – and this was the relief party.

It consisted of two English R.A.M.C. orderlies and about a dozen native porters. The senior orderly examined me and prescribed a nightcap, so a bottle of brandy was uncorked and I slipped off to sleep again. It was nearly 10 a.m. before I awoke. I had a temperature of 102 degrees and more tummy pains, so I was given only a pint of chicken broth.

The orderlies told me that there was a motor ambulance waiting on the far side of the Mgeta River, which was between us and Dethumi, and which they said they thought had overflowed its banks for several miles. I told them that I knew it had. So I left the village on a stretcher with my temperature still at 102 degrees.

We had to cross the Mgeta River by two creeper ropes, one for the hands and one for the feet, which were fixed to a tree on each side. Only one of us could cross at a time, and in the centre the creeper rope sagged to within three feet of the river, which was alive with crocodiles. It was a bit of a teaser, but the passage was safely made and by nightfall I was bathed and between the sheets in the hospital at Dethumi.

Ragged nerves for a bit and a bout of malaria were the only ill-effects, but perhaps I might add even now I am very prejudiced indeed against any holiday suggestion which has to do with 'camping out'.

IX

BOMBING ENGLAND

By KAPITÄNLEUTNANT A. D. JOACHIM
BREITHAUPT

BREITHAUPT, JOACHIM JUSTUS. Born 1883 in Brandenburg. Entered the Imperial Marine in 1903, and promoted as Under-officer 1906. Has commanded warships, torpedo boats and survey ships in the South Seas, Australia and Tsing-Tan. During the War was transferred to the Marine Airship Department and posted to the command of Airship L 6 and L 15, making many reconnaissances and mining expeditions to the North Sea. He was in the great engagement near Terschelling and in the bombing attacks on London in 1915, on Sheffield and Liverpool in 1916 and on London, March 31st, 1916. On the last occasion he was shot down over Rainham and forced to descend at the mouth of the Thames. He was made a prisoner until the end of the War.

In 1919 he was Company commander in the Ehrhardt Brigade at the capture of Munich. Since then he has managed a national newspaper and engaged in business.

In May 1930, he went with the Graf Zeppelin to South America and from Rio Janeiro to New York. He is an expert on the building of airships and airship transport and has edited *With Count Zeppelin to South and North America*.

He has been given the Iron Cross, 1st Class, a medal for life-saving at sea, and other decorations.

BOMBING ENGLAND

BEFORE THE WAR I WAS in England twice, but I saw London for the first time during the War. I saw it then under uncommon circumstances, for in autumn 1915, I was captain of the Zeppelin L 15, and was flying at 10,000 feet above the city, which lay like a map below me.

I should like to think that I am more welcome here now than I was then, even though I have come to remind you of those days by describing my experiences in this series of 'Hazards'. Some of you may perhaps consider this as – how do you say? – adding insult to injury, but I think it is hardly necessary for me to affirm that such is not my wish, or to revive wantonly old grievances and disputes. The War between us has now been over a great many years. I hope that much is forgotten and the rest forgiven between us. It is because I am sure it is that I am going to tell you my experiences as a Zeppelin commander. I am going to describe the experiences and feelings of myself and my crew, and not the damage which it was then our duty to try to inflict.

It is little known that the German fleet had only a single airship at the beginning of the War, the L 3. But from 1914 until 1918 the Friedrichshaven works built sixty Zeppelins for the Navy besides nine Schutte-Lanz ships. Fourteen of these were shot down in land attacks, and four over the sea were so hit by shrapnel that they could not return. Two were destroyed in their sheds by English fliers, thirty were wrecked because of unfavourable circumstances or burnt in their sheds. Some were discarded as being out of date, and so only a few airships existed towards the end of the War.

In the first days August 1914, I was sent to the school for air-shippers in Leipzig, where I got my air pilot's certificate from the old Count Zeppelin in March 1915. Soon after this I was appointed captain of the L 6, which was stationed at Hage, near Norderney, and in September 1915, I became captain of a more capable airship, L 15, and on board this I made my first trip to England.

On October 13, five Zeppelins had risen at noon, and at about 6 p.m. were standing in the face of the clearly visible English coast. The surf shone in the distance, and the rocky outlines were clear against the starry sky. We flew over sea out of sight of the advance trawler and destroyer posts till darkness fell, then we separated, emptied all unnecessary water-ballast bags and steered straight for our chosen objective at the greatest possible height.

Our chief of the naval airships, Commander Strasser, had given us only general directions, for it was impossible for him to judge the weather and local conditions in England from the distant German centre.

I had chosen London. As soon as I reached the English coast L 15 was shot at violently by the batteries and lighted up by searchlights. We sailed on and fixed our position from time to time by throwing out flares; but we did not like to use many of these treacherous lights, since they gave away our own position.

At about 8 p.m. we reached the Thames, which was easy

Captured Zeppelin crew member of the Imperial German Navy Zeppelin LZ 48 known as L 15 – Colin Waters: Alamy Stock Photo.

to recognize on account of her characteristic windings, and the last ballast was dropped to give us the greatest possible height. Everybody was now at his alarm post.

At first London lay almost dark beneath us, but we could make out several points like Regent's Park and the Serpentine. We were being shot at all the time, and when we were flying over the northern suburb of Tottenham the curtain-fire increased, so we decided to attempt the attack from another side.

A sea of houses was now clearly visible beneath us, for the alarm had been given and numerous searchlights had been turned on. We stood out to the west and steered over the suburbs in the direction of the City. It was a beautiful sight to see the shrapnel bursting, though sometimes it came unpleasantly close. On either side the other airships stood against the sky lighted up, like ours, by the beams of the searchlights, and above us twinkled the stars in the clear sky.

We had no eye for the scenic effect, however, and could not think of the feelings of the people; only later on we became conscious of all that. We must concentrate on the events of the moment and make decisions as quick as lightning. We had to change our course very often to avoid the much too obtrusive searchlight beams and the bursting shrapnel.

I should have liked to go higher up, but my ship was already as high as it would go. As we crossed Waterloo Bridge the variometer indicated about 11,000 feet. We had counted on a lower temperature and, therefore, a better carrying power of the air. All we could do in this hellfire that protected London was to stick to it and to trust to luck. I cannot, of course, tell what was the effect of the bombs we dropped in the heart of your City: at any rate, they frequently started large fires in the places where they fell.

Some of your excellent historians confirm my observations of that time. They state that my ship was flying exactly above the City, from Exeter Street to Farringdon Street. They say that my bombs did serious damage along the line from Hyde Park, Charing Cross, Strand, Lincoln's Inn, Chancery Lane, Hatton Garden, Houndsditch, Aldgate and Limehouse; 2,000 kg bombs were dropped, and a long strip of fire beneath and behind us showed clearly the effect of our work.

Our intended targets were the Admiralty and the Bank of England, but if we failed to hit them the newspaper quarter at Ludgate Hill did not seem less worth trying for. According to newspaper reports two of my bombs damaged the front of the *Morning Post* office.

In this way, after an hour's sharp firing, we crossed the City and left it behind us. But suddenly we were fired at violently from an unexpected direction. At the same time the look-out on the back of the ship shouted through the speaking tube that English aeroplanes were darting through the rays of the searchlights above and beside us. Light grenades and flares tore through the air. We could follow their course as clearly as on a drawing so that we were able to avoid them. At last after an hour of exciting life the City lay far behind us and my men heaved a sigh of relief.

We were fired at once more over the coast, but without effect. We were out of range, I think. Then, as a farewell we dropped our last bombs on a searchlight battery.

At midnight we were 12,000 feet high over the sea, and steering for home by way of the Dutch coast. When we were near Terschelling at about 5 a.m. a nasty fog appeared. We took our bearings by wireless, but it was difficult to make out our position. However, we must find the landing-place as soon as possible, for we were already short of fuel and two of the motors were working irregularly.

Five hours later we sighted through the fog the top of a church which we thought to be Bremen. We couldn't risk going lower than two hundred feet, and the surface of the ground was still quite invisible. We reckoned that we ought to be near the landing-place at about noon, but now our third motor did not work either, and I had only a single one left. At last the long expected captive balloon appeared just before us over the foggy clouds. This was the way by which the landing-place was marked in misty weather.

I at once forced my way through the fog, but at the same moment my last motor refused to work. The ship lost driving power and rose again to 1,500 feet. The southern winds drove it like a drifting balloon over the impenetrable clouds to the sea, so I decided to try my luck and to land immediately. I opened the gas valves, and the ship was made heavier than the surrounding air. It fell at first slowly, then more and more quickly, and the variometer indicated a descent of twenty feet a second. It was a nervous business, as we hadn't a bit of ballast at our disposal to diminish our rate of fall.

Down we went. At a hundred feet we saw the ground again for the first time in ten hours. Immediately afterwards we struck it heavily. The gondola was pressed into the framework, but we escaped with light wounds though we were violently knocked about.

We had been extremely lucky. There were no trees or houses round us, and the L 15 was drifting slowly in a soft wind over a far-stretching heath. Part of the crew alighted at once and hung on to it to anchor it, while others were sent to reconnoitre. They discovered that we were five kilometres away from the landing-place. People from a near village were employed to assist, and after about two hours several hundred sailors of the airship station arrived in motor cars in reply to our telephone call.

Under great difficulties L 15 was brought into the shed. Trees and telegraph posts that were in its way had to be felled and a group of pioneers marched in front of us and cut a way through the woods. Our chief, Commander Strasser, received us full of joy. He had known all the difficulties of our situation, and had been anxiously awaiting our return since dawn. We were the last to arrive. I received the Iron Cross for this trip, and my whole crew got the second class of the Cross.

My second attack on England was directed at the Western industrial district. On a foggy night in January 1916, I flew for almost eight hours in zigzag courses over the Midlands, looking in vain for suitable targets. I wanted to reach Liverpool, but according to the English historians I only reached Burton-on-Trent. This trip was extremely difficult, not only on account of complicated navigation, but because my only compass refused to work, so we had to steer with the help of the stars.

Two months later I took part in a squadron attack of five ships on England. On the evening of March 30, 1916, the chief rang up the senior captain and gave these orders:

'In case of constant weather all available airships shall rise tomorrow to attack Middle and South England. Chief objectives are London and the industrial districts, Lincoln,

Scene showing the wrecked Zeppelin L15 airship, sunk off the mouth of the Thames – Trinity Mirror – Mirrorpix: Alamy Stock Photo.

Nottingham and Derby. Rise so that the English coast will be reached at dawn.'

We hear the gay voice of the senior captain, Captain Matthy, answering. We sit in the club for a while and discuss the situation, and then we separate to give the necessary orders for the coming day to the officers of the watch, the pilots and the engineers.

By dawn the landing-place is full of life. The doors of the sheds are open, the motors start with a growl for a few seconds' trial run. Benzine, gas and ballast water are poured in through hose pipes. Fire bombs and high explosive bombs are wheeled to the ships on heavy barrows. At about II a.m. the weather conditions are once more discussed with the chief, and he gives the order to rise. Whistles and horn signals sound the 'stand-to' to the five hundred men who staff the aerodrome, the ships' crews go on board, officers of the watch inform the captains that the ships are 'ready to start!' and the air conditions in the higher regions are tested once more by aid of weather report and pilot balloons.

The order 'Airship, march!' is given, and one ship after another is pulled with ropes out of the shed on to the aerodrome. The greatest care must be taken, as the slightest touch of the light framework against the walls of the shed would be of the greatest consequence. By repeated careful weighing off, that is by letting out water, the airship, which is now held by only a few men, is made lighter than air. The side motors begin to growl, and at the command 'Up!' L 15 rises by the bow majestically into the air.

Over the Frisian Isles we steer, keeping low and well away from the Dutch coast to avoid any infringement of neutrality. A thick fog covers the sea. Even at two hundred feet we can no longer see the ground. We avoid inquisitive, invisible watchers by getting behind the 'washhouse' as the air-skipper calls the moist masses of clouds.

At 2,000 feet it gets clear. What a lovely sight! Beneath us impenetrable fog, above us a blue sky and glorious sunshine! It is impossible for anyone who has not seen it to imagine this unforgettable picture. Among the mountains and valleys formed by clouds on which the golden sun is reflected the ship steers a safe course. We seem to stand on top of a high mountain surrounded by white gleaming glaciers, and here and there among the clouds another airship appears on the same errand as ours. Ten airships are steering westwards, waving greetings and 'good luck' to each other. Hidden by the fog and without incident we draw close to the English coast.

All at once at about 6 p.m. the clouds clear. Dark spots beneath us are recognized as the sea. We must be getting very near the English advanced posts.

I now increase my height. The ship drops ballast and rises slowly, three thousand, five thousand feet. Everybody goes to his alarm post, and the bombs are got ready to be dropped.

At 7.30 p.m. lights begin to show behind us now and then the beams of a searchlight that explores the sky for anything dangerous. They come from the guardships, that are probably alarmed by the noise of the motors. Surely the English, with their wonderfully organized spy service, know already of our visit. The helmsman makes out our position as far as he can from the terrestrial objects that are visible.

Till night falls we keep over the sea. We drop the last ballast that is at our disposal at 8 p.m. The instruments show nine thousand feet and we feel the rise too for the cold increases.

We are fired at sharply by English batteries as we pass the coast, and some strong searchlights manage to light up the ship at moments. Then it gets pitch dark.

Since my first visit the English have learned how to screen their lights. At that time one could see lighted trains, and partly illuminated villages. But today England is asleep, though with strained nerves, in expectance of coming events. Our former visits have had their effect.

We are forced now and then to drop a lightbomb to fix our position. Its split-stars illuminate the country under us dazzlingly for one minute. Our goal is London, and this time we know our way better. The airship steers a course southwards to the Thames and then turns westwards. At about 11 p.m. we calculate to have reached the border of London, but there is nothing to see of the city for a long time.

Suddenly searchlights spring out. Their rays search the sky hastily, first singly, then in groups. Presently one picks out our dark gondola and examines it closely. Others follow. Guns open fire on us. Shrapnels are bursting on either side, above us, under us. They pass our ship in elegant parabolic curves. A short look at the map, a few words to the helmsman, and the speaking tubes call 'Clear for action!' into all parts of the ship.

The officer of the watch lies on his stomach looking through the pendulum telescope; the sentries on the platform are eagerly scanning the sky for fliers. They report their observations through the speaking tube to the pilot in the gondola.

The shells are coming closer and closer. We are now hit several times in the middle part of the ship, and the steering-gear is put out of action. But by some miracle the L 15 did not catch fire.

I investigated the damage. Four gas bags had been emptied and the carrying capacity was therefore greatly reduced. I thought I would try to reach Ostend, but in a slow even curve the ship sank from 12,000 to 2,000 feet. For a long time a flier accompanied us, but he did not manage to attain our height and lost us. Our machine-guns fired sharply, but at last they had to be dropped with all our metal parts to make the ship lighter. Above Ipswich the batteries fired once more, but without effect; then we were over the sea.

When the first well-aimed broadsides of exploding shrapnel burst on all sides and fliers visible only for a moment darted through the rays of the searchlights I suppose each man of the crew had the feeling of momentary danger. The captain who bears the responsibility is especially conscious of the seriousness of the situation, as he has to give his orders as quick as lightning. But he has too much to do to be frightened. He has to change the course frequently to avoid the dangerous districts and he has to find the best targets for the bombs.

I think I can truthfully say that what with giving orders and listening to hasty information I myself was not conscious

Artist's depiction of Zeppelin raid on London in May 1915.

of any danger. Even when information came of the first hits and we saw the dire consequences; even when the ship had an inclination at the bow of thirty degrees and we could not keep it steering steadily any longer, there was no time for feeling.

These were minutes of the highest nerve tension. I had to reach the open sea as soon as possible, not only to get out of danger, but because to fall on land would have given useful parts of the framework into the hands of the enemy. This had to be avoided, the more as L 15 was the first ship which had been shot down over England.

Every man of my excellent crew worked feverishly, dropping all weights overboard. Our important secret maps and papers had also to be destroyed so that they might not fall into the enemy's hands. Only when all imaginable orders for the saving of ship and men were given and the call for help was signalled in ciphers to the home station stillness fell upon the crew. And in these few moments I saw clearly that we could not even reach the Belgian coast, for the ship was falling evenly all the time. We should be in the sea at any moment.

My chief desire now, more important than saving the crew, was to prevent the enemy getting L 15 even as a wreck. If we could reach the open sea we had the best chance to land 'softly' and destroy the ship. So when the Thames estuary was reached a strong feeling of calmness came over me. At about midnight the L 15, flying at 1,000 feet, doubled in two through loss of gas and fell vertically into the sea.

We were about thirty miles off the coast, when this happened. I was in the gondola, which was entirely submerged and was pushed to and fro by the masses of water that rushed in. Suddenly I came to the surface and was drawn into the ship by the men of my crew. I had foreseen what would

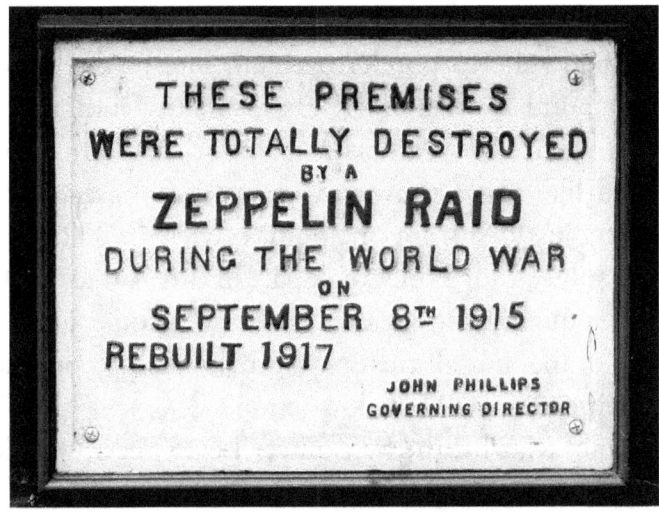

Zeppelin Raid plaque, 61 Farringdon Road, London.

happen, however, and had therefore only kept two men in the gondola; all the others had been sent into the ship, where the bouncing would not be so strong. One of the helmsmen who had been at my side never came up again; the other had all his teeth knocked out. I escaped with concussion and several light wounds.

The L 15 was now sinking. The crew were on top of the ship and its middle part was covered by water.

Half an hour passed and then a trawler came near us; we called for a boat, but the trawler went off again. Sometime later four trawlers appeared on the other side of the ship, about one hundred yards away. While we waited, we cut the gas bags and opened the valves to ensure the sinking of the ship and that the English should not get her.

The succeeding events do not belong to my theme. At first we were taken on board the trawler *Oliwiene*; then on to the destroyer *Vulture*, which brought us to Chatham. Later on we had time to ponder over our fate in the Detention Barracks, and from there I was taken to Donington Hall, where I spent two years with many other German officers. I should like to say, however, in conclusion, that I do not really feel justified from one point of view in talking to you on this subject, for I only took part in three attacks. Officers of higher quality and greater experience should be speaking instead of me, but all the best German airship commanders and their crews were killed in action.

Captain Matthy, the best officer I ever knew, who led his airship sixteen times to England, met his fate on October 1, 1916, over Cheshunt; Lieutenant Tempest with his aeroplane brought him down. My good leader, Commander Strasser, on board his L 70, was also brought down over England in August 1918.

The few who got through to the end, such as Captain-Lieutenant Dietrich, suffered severely in health on account of the increasing strain imposed upon them of flying at more than 20,000 feet in temperatures of thirty to forty degrees below zero. So I speak to you not because I was one of our most experienced and important Zeppelin commanders, but because it so happened that I was preserved by being shot down early and taken prisoner.

Some people think that Germany could have reduced whole cities to ashes by a more definite and concentrated use of her airships. In my opinion this would have been impossible even in 1914–15, when you had little anti-aircraft defence, and later on, of course, your English fliers by their excellent bravery greatly reduced the Zeppelin danger. Under the influence of war nerves the English people began by overrating the effect of airship attacks, and the Press did all it could to exaggerate the imaginary dangers so as to force the Government to take up energetic measures of defence for the alarmed population.

But the German authorities always knew the limited possibilities of airship attacks and they never expected them to have any decisive influence upon the course of the war. At the same time, however, they did not underrate their moral effect. The right of using bomb dropping Zeppelins has been greatly disputed, but I do not intend to discuss this matter, or whether it is fairer to drop bombs on enemy cities to the risk of the civil population or deliberately to starve them by sea blockades. That is war, and in war every country will say that it has the right and the duty to do everything it can to secure its own endangered existence.

X

TEN THOUSAND MILES IN THE SADDLE

By A. F. TSCHIFFELY

TSCHIFFELY, A. F., is by birth Swiss-Argentine. He started life as a schoolmaster and, after being educated and teaching in England, he went to the Argentine.

He spent most of his spare time in that country travelling on horseback in the pampas.

He has made several expeditions into the wilds of Northern Argentina.

TEN THOUSAND MILES IN THE SADDLE

IT WASN'T JUST MADNESS, OR a desire for publicity that induced me to ride two horses from the extreme south of South America to the United States when comfortable ships would have taken me from point to point in three weeks, or less.

The two horses I took with me were descendants of the stock which was shipped to South America by the Spanish Conquistadores, about four hundred years ago. Many of them were turned loose by the Spaniards and others managed to escape during hostile attacks by the Indians. But owing to various circumstances this wild breed of horses was becoming nearly extinct, and the object of my ride was to prove to the Government that it was hardy and useful, and worth saving from extinction.

My journey took me two and a half years and was probably the longest expedition ever made on horseback.

I travelled over vast plains, through deserts, jungles, swamps and over lofty mountains. In one place in the Andes we were close on 18,000 feet above sea level, and then again we found ourselves in steaming tropical swamps and jungles where it was often necessary to use a bush-knife to open a trail through the dense vegetation. I say 'we' although I was travelling without human companionship, for after all my two faithful horses did most of the hard work, and if it hadn't been for their instincts and thinking I should have come to grief on more than one occasion.

I had to go down to the far south of the Argentine Republic to find them, for I wanted a couple of animals which would be able to stand so long and arduous an expedition. There I bought thirty horses from a Tehuelche Indian Chief named Liempichun, which means 'I have feathers', and when they had been driven I chose two which looked good and tough to me.

Although they were sixteen and eighteen years old respectively, neither of these horses had ever been ridden, and you can imagine what kind of a war-dance they led me when I first jumped on to their backs. Rodeo horses may be showy goat-jumpers, but for real unadulterated buck-jumping I recommend the hurricane deck of a wild horse. However, after a great deal of patience and kindness on my part, and one or two nasty falls, the horses became more friendly, and I was ready to start.

I had spent something like two years studying the road I proposed to follow, and had gathered as much information about the different countries as I could. This, incidentally, was very little and vague, as I found out later.

Although I tried to avoid publicity the Press soon heard about my proposed journey, and the comments were many and varied. Most of the papers thought the trip was impossible, and one or two said frankly that I ought to consult a doctor. Others were of the opinion that the expedition involved cruelty to animals. If these worthy gentlemen of the Press had only thought a little they might have realized that if a man sets out into the wilds with two horses, his life will depend on them to a great extent, and he will make it his first duty to attend to their welfare.

Usually I rode on one horse while the other carried the pack, and I changed from one to the other whenever I thought the change would do them good. When the trail was steep, or the going difficult, I divided the pack between them and went on foot, for the horses made faster progress in this way and there was less danger of a nasty fall. Although I had to sleep out in the open very often I could not carry a tent, for even the lightest would have meant extra weight for the packhorse. I often had to sleep in huts, but I much preferred to curl up somewhere in the open where there were fewer insects than are to be found in most of the habitations of Indians and half-breeds.

I rarely bothered about wild beasts, for most of them are afraid of man and are only too glad to keep out of his way.

Tschiffely (second from right) during his epic journey by horseback.

Crushed garlic, rubbed on a rope made of horsehair, will usually keep snakes away from a sleeping man if he places this rope in a circle around him before he lies down to sleep on the ground. The only beast of prey which might attack a man in South or Central America is the jaguar, but since it isn't found in many places, one is fairly safe.

I have read in books and heard travellers tell how they made fires all night to keep pumas away. The puma is the American lion; in North America they often call him 'cougar'. This animal is very cowardly, but rather curious and, after all, if the nervous traveller wishes to make fires all night one can hardly blame the poor puma for that. No; the real dangers I had to face were lack of water and food; and dangerous trails in the mountains. Then there were burning deserts and steaming tropical swamps, and the possibility of fever and sickness.

I once had to stay for four days in a filthy settlement where over 150 natives were down with bubonic plague, and during my stay in the place twenty-four died of this horrible disease.

The swimming of torrential mountain rivers also presents many hazards, and in some of the tropical waters one has to look out for alligators and crocodiles. Even worse than these are the small cannibal fish, called carribes or pirhanas. They attack in thousands and will tear to pieces in a few seconds any human being or animal which happens to have a cut or scratch, for they are attracted by the smell of blood.

Another unpleasant customer which lurks in some of the muddy waters is an ugly flat fish: the poisonous stinging ray. The tremblador or electric eel, one of nature's most extraordinary freaks, is another very dangerous denizen of some tropical streams and rivers.

The discharge of one of these living electric batteries is powerful enough to paralyse a horse and cause him to sink like lead. They are from three to five feet long and about as thick as a man's arm. As well as poisonous fish, all sorts of different poisonous herbs and weeds grow in some parts of South America, and they will kill a horse if he eats them. I came across several varieties of these herbs, and had to take great care that my animals did not get them.

From Buenos Aires we set out in a north-westerly direction towards the distant Bolivian border. There are few roads in that mountainous country, so I had carefully planned to arrive in Bolivia during the dry season; for I knew that the only means of communication would be the dry river beds. I had plenty of time, so I took things easy. But I had no end of trouble with the horses for the first few days, for they were none too tame and shied at such things as houses and traffic, which they had never seen in their desolate native regions in the far south. As soon as we were out in the open pampas things became more pleasant, and Mancha and Gato – as I had called the horses – gradually became more friendly. Mancha means 'spot' and Gato 'cat'.

I had two .45 calibre six-shooters strapped to my hips, and the packhorse also carried a .44 rifle and a 16-bore repeating shotgun, for I knew I would have to rely a good deal on firearms for food. The type of saddle I used was a light framework of wood covered with leather. I piled sheepskins on this, and was able to use it as a comfortable bed as well as for riding.

We jogged along for days over the vast flatness, which suggested eternity. There was little wild life to be seen except prairie owls and other birds. Herds of cattle were grazing, and occasionally a *gaucho*, or Argentine cattle boy, passed us.

It got warmer as we continued north, and when we entered the huge alkali flats the sun rays seemed to penetrate to the very bones. The water is so scarce and bad there, and the place is so barren, excepting for a few cactus plants and other shrubs, that I had been told that I should never get my horses across. But we managed all right and, when we came out safe and sound on the other side, I was well satisfied with my animals, for they had given the first real proof of their toughness. At length we entered the mighty Andes, and travelled for days through vast valleys, using the dry river beds as roads, and guessing our direction with more luck than judgment.

As we approached the Bolivian border, we occasionally met Indians who were on their way down to distant villages or towns. Once a year – during the dry season – the hardy mountaineers make their long journeys. Their woven goods and beautifully made pottery are packed on llamas, the pretty and elegant South American beasts of burden, which they drive before them. When they have sold or exchanged their goods they return home before the rains set in and the wild rivers thunder down the deep ravines and canyons, on their way to the distant Atlantic.

The further we penetrated into this vast and imposing labyrinth of mountains the rougher and less hospitable the country became. Icy blasts swept down from the high peaks, and there was nothing green to be seen. For days we stumbled over rocks and boulders in river beds, and sometimes we threaded our way along giddy precipices where the horses had to pick their way with the greatest care.

It was bitterly cold in the high passes, and mountain sickness

– caused by the low air pressure – sometimes made my nose bleed profusely and caused a feeling of giddiness. This mountain sickness – called *sorroche* or *puna* in the Andes – often affects animals as well, and, unless the traveller takes care never to over-exert his mount, it may collapse and even die.

The natives in some of these regions have a very rough, but quite effective cure for it. If one of their animals falls, they quickly cut a gash in the roof of its mouth to bleed it, and then blow a little pure alcohol up its nostrils. I never hurried my horses where the trails were steep, and gave them a rest whenever they asked for it and I assure you that once a horse gets used to a man, he learns how to ask for many things.

In many parts of Bolivia it is advisable not to drink water. It looks clear enough, but it is often bad and even dangerous. The natives make themselves a strong alcoholic beverage with corn. This abounds wherever Indians live, and its preparation is original, though not very appetising. First of all, a quantity of corn is boiled for some hours, and in the meantime more corn is chewed by the Indians. When it has been masticated into a soft paste and well mixed with saliva, they spit it into a wooden bowl. The resulting paste is called *moco*, and acts rather as yeast does in the making of bread. When the boiled corn is ready, the chewed *moco* is added to it, and soon the concoction begins to fizz and bubble, and after a day or so the native beer, or *chicha*, is ready. Owing to the scarcity of good water, I had to drink quite a lot of *chicha* – and what the eye has seen the heart can grieve over.

After weeks of travelling, we reached La Paz, the capital of Bolivia, and shortly afterwards a bloody uprising broke out in the Indian territory which we had just left, and many whites lost their lives. In most cases my sympathy goes to the poor and oppressed Indians, who have suffered untold injustices and misery ever since the Spaniards, under Pizarro, invaded their land.

We continued north from La Paz, skirted Lake Titicaca, and finally reached Curco, the ancient capital of the Inca Empire. This lake is some 14,000 feet above sea level and, although it does not look very big on the map, it took me a week to ride along its full length, from south to north. In this neighbourhood we passed several most interesting ruins, which date back to Incaic and pre-Incaic times, and, although I am a keen student of archaeology, I could not stay in these regions as long as I would like to have done. From there we swung due west and entered another terrific network of mountains – frightfully rough country where nature works on so gigantic a scale that it often made me gasp.

When we were on the mountaintops it was bitterly cold, and when we had stumbled down over neck-breaking trails into steaming tropical valleys, swarms of mosquitoes attacked us, whilst flocks of parrots screeched as if protesting against our invasion. Sometimes we had to cross Indian hanging bridges across deep chasms. When we came to the first of these hammock – like structures, which sagged dangerously in the middle, I thought my horses would never get across it, but the animals picked their way with great care, and when the bridge swayed too much they stopped until it was safe to proceed. Some of these bridges were only about three feet wide, and I always unsaddled the horses and took them across singly, for I did not think these wobbly and giddy pieces of primitive engineering would have stood the weight of two horses. I sometimes feared that one animal would be too much for these frail but daring constructions.

Once, while we were following a narrow trail, one of the horses lost his foothold and shot down a steep incline to what looked like certain death. Luckily, however, his descent was stopped by a solitary tree on the very edge of a deep precipice. It was not at all an easy job to rescue him, but he seemed to realize the danger for he never moved until ropes and lassos had been tied to him and he had been pulled back to safety with the assistance of friendly Indians.

Eventually we reached Lima, the capital of Peru. This old city is situated near the shores of the Pacific Ocean, and from there we continued North along the coast.

We had to travel through sandy deserts where the heat was terrific. It never rains in these coastal regions, and water can only be found where rivers come down from the Andes. One desert which we had to cross was ninety-six miles from river to river; a dangerous journey which took us twenty hours to accomplish. We did most of the travelling at night, but, since we could only do this when there was a moon to help us, we often had to forge ahead during the daytime, when the tropical sun baked the sand to such a degree that I could feel it burn through my heavy riding boots.

Often I rode for miles over the wet sands along the beach where thousands of sea birds circled above us. The monotony of the scenery and the regular breaking of the waves often made me feel very sleepy, and I found it very difficult to keep awake. When we came nearer to the equator, I again changed the route and took to the mountains once more. It was cooler there, though the broken country made progress very slow. But I had had enough of deserts, heat and quicksands along the Peruvian coast, and had no desire to attempt crossing the low swamp land along the coast of Ecuador.

Up and down wound our trail, sometimes through dense vegetation in hot, tropical valleys, where the horses had to wade through deep mud, and where we had to be on the look-out for mud holes. These and quicksands are very dangerous traps; they are extremely difficult to distinguish from the rest of the ground, and should the traveller happen to blunder on to one of them he will be sucked down and perish unless help is at hand.

Once the horse I was riding refused to go a step further, and the more I tried to urge him on the fussier he became. When I finally used my spurs, he reared up and snorted, but still refused to go forward. Luckily an Indian who spoke Spanish appeared on the scene and told me that I was on the very edge of a dangerous mud hole. How my horse sensed the danger is really mysterious, for there were none of these mud holes in his native regions. He probably saved my life, anyway, for I remember how a mounted guide, who once worked for me, trod on one of these places. His pony at once sank in, and if I had not carried lassos and ropes it would never have got free. As it was, we had a very difficult and exciting time pulling the poor beast out.

I was very proud and pleased when we crossed the equator, not far from Quito, the capital of Ecuador. Strange as it may seem, it was very cool there, for we were high above sea level, and near us towered several beautiful snow-capped peaks and volcanoes, their snows glittering in the dark blue sky.

The Indians in every region through which we passed varied a lot in dress and general appearance, and many were the languages they spoke. If they did not understand any Spanish I had to make myself understood by signs, and this was often none too easy, and required a great deal of patience.

Tschiffely scans the horizon in Ecuador.

Colombia was not an easy nut to crack, but we finally reached the shores of the Caribbean Sea at the extreme north of South America. We had been on the road just about one year. The rainy season had now set in, and in many places we had to do almost as much swimming as walking at least, so it seemed to me at the time. Once, during a severe thunderstorm, I was knocked off my mount and stunned by a flash of lightning, but luckily I was not much hurt.

The overland trip from the north of Colombia to Panama is impossible because of swamps and impenetrable jungles, and so I was obliged to embark the horses as far as Cristobal, near the Panama Canal. We stayed hereabouts for nearly a month and a half – about the longest stay I made anywhere – until the rains subsided and the jungles had dried up. Then I saddled up and set out again towards the forests and dense jungles which lie between Panama and Costa Rica. For several weeks we fought our way through dense vegetation and dark forests. We had to cross an 11,000-foot mountain range from which I could see both the Pacific and Atlantic Oceans, and the jungles below us looked like another angry sea of green.

In some parts it was very difficult to find food, and I often fed off parrots, wild turkeys, woodpigeons and similar birds, and occasionally a wild pig provided me with meat. But I was once so hard up for food that I had to shoot and eat monkeys, though it made me feel like a common murderer, and the meat was extremely tough. My menu was often a strange one, and among other rare dishes I have had to eat large lizards, or iguanas as they are called in Latin America; crocodile, horse meat, ostrich eggs, armadillo, and even a snake once figured on my bill of fare. The latter tasted rather like a mixture of chicken and fish, and in some parts it is considered a delicacy by the native gourmets. The horses had their share of strange fodder, too, for grass does not grow everywhere. They also provided unwilling food for others, for in the jungles, ticks, vampire bats and many other pests made life unpleasant for them. Some of the South American vampire bats are much bigger than the useful European bats, and, though they never bothered me, I had no end of trouble when they attacked my horses. The big ones can suck as much as half a pint of blood, and if a few of these repulsive creatures get at a horse they weaken him terribly. But I soon found a way of protecting my two pets against vampires and ticks, and managed to keep them healthy and strong.

What with jungles and revolutions, I had plenty of excitement in Central America, and later, when I thought the rest of the journey would be just plain sailing, I ran into more revolutions in Mexico, where I had a very lively time of it. Fighting and banditry obliged me to make a big detour over the mountains, and, in spite of the delay caused by this, we slowly approached our goal. I soon found out that a pleasant smile will take a man further than all the guns will, and somehow I managed to wriggle through without worse consequences than a black eye and a bullet through my saddle sheepskin.

When things became too hot, the Mexican Government provided me with military escorts who accompanied me through the most dangerous parts. Long before I had reached that country, the authorities and people knew about my ride, and since Mexicans are keen horsemen and lovers of the open, our long journey appealed to them, and they saw to it that nothing should happen to us on our way through their beautiful but turbulent country. After we had crossed the Rio Grande into Texas, things were easy, but the further we went the heavier the traffic became. Finally, I unsaddled in New York, and we took a ship back to the Argentine.

Thanks to delays caused by an official reception, I missed sailing on the ill-fated *Vestris* which sank, with over a hundred lives lost. We left the United States in the next boat, and you may be sure that I did not leave my two horses behind, but took them back home with me on a comfortable passenger liner.

Thus they lived again to see their beloved pampas, where they were turned loose to roam from horizon to horizon and enjoy the life that is natural to them. They have done their duty!

THE 'HAZARD' BROADCASTS

Written records of the original broadcasts in 1932, which provide the content for this book, still exist courtesy of the Radio Times and the BBC 'Genome' Archive. Sadly no recordings of the various speakers remain.

We have included the original programme listings as they appeared in The Radio Times. Unfortunately, there is no record of the content of HAZARD XI and interestingly HAZARD IX is not included in the original book; all we have is the summary. There appear to be no extant records of the broadcast itself although the exploits of Harry St John Philby, father of spy Kim Philby, are well documented in his many books about Arabia.

'HAZARD' I

First broadcast: Sat 21st May 1932, 21:20 on National Programme Daventry

Rear-Admiral E. R. G. R. Evans, CB, DSO: 'Antarctic Sledging with Captain Scott'

This is the first in a series of personal narratives dealing with moments of peril in peace and war, somewhat on the lines of the 'Escape' series broadcast last summer. That flair for adventure which has always characterized Rear-Admiral E. R. G. R. Evans must have led him into many tight corners, any one of which would make a memorable story. He might have described his part in the bombardment of the German line from the Belgian coast very early in the war – or his more famous exploit in 1917 while in command of HMS *Broke* of the Dover Patrol, when that boat and HMS *Swift* engaged and defeated six German destroyers. However, he has chosen as his 'big thrill' to recount some of his Antarctic experiences. As he was second in command to Captain R. F. Scott in the expedition of 1910–11 which ended so tragically with Scott's death, he may be said to know those grim Antarctic regions at their very grimmest.

Contributor
Rear-Admiral E. R. G. R. Evans

'HAZARD' II

First broadcast: Sat 28th May 1932, 21:20 on National Programme Daventry

Mr G. W. T. Garrood, A.F.C. (late RAF): 'Lost in the African Jungle'

Mr Garrood was the hero of one of the many thrilling 'hazards' born of war in the air. Forced down in the jungle, he was lost for four days, had his clothes stolen by baboons, was attacked by a crocodile and spent a night of enforced imprisonment up a tree with a leopard underneath. The adventures of a German Zeppelin commander follow in this series next week.

Contributor
Mr. G. W. T. Garrood

'HAZARD' III

First broadcast: Sat 4th Jun 1932, 21:20 on National Programme Daventry

Kapitänleutnant a. D. Joachim Breithaupt: 'Zeppelin Raid on London'

It is a truism that prolonged danger and strain often demand a higher type of courage than the running of a momentary risk. Kapitanleutnant Breithaupt commanded the German Zeppelin unit L 15 during the Great War, and was on board when his airship was forced down in the North Sea. His talk will describe the ordeal of a Zeppelin Commander, and reveal much that is not known of the intensity of that ordeal. The hazards of war are common to men on both sides, and the telling of them can only serve the cause of union. The adventures of a British submarine officer will be the next contribution to this symposium.

Contributor
Kapitänleutnant a. D. Joachim Breithaupt

'HAZARD' IV

First broadcast: Sat 11th Jun 1932, 21:00 on National Programme Daventry

Commander H. G. Stoker, DSO, RN

Men will never, so long as memory of the war endures, cease to dispute the tactical wisdom of the Dardanelles venture, but the manner of its conduct can never be disputed. It was a magnificent 'hazard,' involving far more than personal risks. Commander Stoker was in command of the first submarine to forge the passage of the Dardanelles; he was also taken prisoner. The tale of his experiences will recall the risks run by every man who took part in that adventure. Commander Stoker is the author of that thrilling play *Below the Surface*, in which the ordeal of an imprisoned submarine crew is movingly portrayed, so his broadcast story should lose nothing by the manner of its telling.

Contributor
H. G. Stoker

'HAZARD' V

First broadcast: Sat 18th Jun 1932, 21:20 on National Programme Daventry

Weathering a Storm with Mr Weston Martyr

Mr Weston Martyr, whose life-long hobby it has been to sail little boats about big seas, has an unusual hazard to relate, and an unusual way of telling it. He will take each of his listeners as shipmates on a 300-mile voyage in a 30-foot schooner from the coast of Nova Scotia to Massachusetts. Together they will experience some of the thrills – high winds, mountainous seas, fire in the cabin, grounding in the shallows – that come to the adventurer in tiny ships.

Contributor
Mr Weston Martyr

'HAZARD' VI

First broadcast: Sat 25th Jun 1932, 21:20 on National Programme Daventry

Captain Harold Armstrong, OBE: 'Brigand Hunting in Turkey'

Captain Armstrong fought in the siege of Kut under General Townshend, was a prisoner of war in Turkey, and after the war the Assistant Military Attaché to the British Embassy at Constantinople. In 1922 he was put in charge of the Turkish Gendarmerie in Skutari, the district across the Bosphorus from Constantinople. His work here was to break up a particularly fierce band of brigands, who were ravaging the countryside, pillaging, murdering, and making themselves generally unpleasant. Extermination with a small force of horse and foot gendarmerie was a long and hazardous business, and Captain Armstrong's story will make exciting hearing.

Contributor
Captain Harold Armstrong

'HAZARD' VII

First broadcast: Sat 2nd Jul 1932, 21:20 on National Programme Daventry

Admiral Gordon Campbell, VC, DSO, MP: 'Mystery Ships'

'Mystery Ships' or 'Q' Ships as they were for a short time called, came into existence as one of the British defence methods against the German submarine menace. They were apparently harmless merchantmen, but in reality extremely well-armed men-of-war, with a full equipment of guns, and a crew trained to the minute, as a 'U' Boat unwary enough to come to the surface after apparently crippling one by torpedo fire soon discovered. The war at sea had no more dangerous phase than that covered by those ships, whose crews so often had to abandon all chance of rescue in order to make sure of getting their submarine.

Admiral Gordon Campbell commanded three of these ships – HMS *Q5*, HMS *Pargust*, and HMS *Dunraven* – that accounted for enemy submarines in 1917. The *Q5* action was described officially as the supreme test of naval discipline, as it might well be, since the guns' crew had to remain concealed in their gun-houses for nearly half an hour while the ship slowly sank lower in the water.

Contributor
Admiral Gordon Campbell

'HAZARD' VIII

First broadcast: Sat 9th Jul 1932, 21:20 on National Programme Daventry

Commander Ernst Hashagen: 'U Boat'

Last week Admiral Gordon Campbell told in this series the story of the Mystery (Q) Ships' fight against the U-Boat menace. This week Commander Hashagen, a U-Boat commander, recounts his version of the War at sea. In August 1917, he was despatched on a special mission to the Atlantic. Shortage of fuel forced him to return by the Straits of Dover, guarded by an elaborate barrage composed of nets, mines, and sunken vessels. British submarine-chasers, aeroplanes, and destroyers were on his track. His log records his decision, 'to break through on a dark night, the net must be dived under in the deepest channel.' This story of his dash for safety is one of the most thrilling in this exciting series.

Contributor
Ernst Hashagen

'HAZARD' IX

First broadcast: Sat 16th Jul 1932, 21:20 on National Programme Daventry

Mr H. St John Philby: 'Ninety Days in the Desert'

This week's 'hazard' departs from the realm of war exploits and returns to the sustained dangers of exploration and travel in unknown lands. Mr St John Philby has just returned from a memorable journey across the Great Sandy Desert – Rub al Khali – of Arabia. He travelled 1,800 miles in ninety days with only two changes of camels, in search of a great buried city of the sands. He has returned with important knowledge of two ancient historical sites, the course of a once famous river, invaluable mineral and geographical remains, and a traveller's tale of surpassing excitement.

Contributor
Mr H. St John Philby

'HAZARD' X

First broadcast: Sat 23rd Jul 1932, 21:20 on National Programme Daventry

Major P.C. Wren: 'Twenty-four Hours in the Foreign Legion'

Tonight Major P.C. Wren, who has seen service with the British, French, and Indian armies, describes some of his first-hand experiences in that strangely assorted international corps of the French army in Northern Africa – the Foreign Legion. He describes how and why he became a 'legionnaire,' the kind of men who were his comrades, the hazards of a desert march – heat, drought, sandstorms, heavy kit, scarcity of water, and that terrible order, 'March or Die.' His hazard ends with an Arab attack at dawn, the lancers of the desert desperately charging the massed bayonets of the legionaries. The author of 'Beau Geste' with such material can be relied upon for a 'beau broadcast.'

Contributor
Major P.C. Wren

'HAZARD' XI

First broadcast: Sat 30th Jul 1932, 21:20 on National Programme Daventry

www.ingramcontent.com/pod-product-compliance
Lightning Source LLC
Chambersburg PA
CBHW072051110526
44590CB00018B/3124